AMERICA the BEAUTIFUL

MAINE

By Ty Harrington

Consultants

Robert M. York, Ph.D., Maine State Historian; Professor Emeritus, University of Maine

Scott Grant, M. Ed., Founder, Maine Studies Institute; Director, Graduate Education, University of Southern Maine; former Consultant, Social Studies, State Department of Education and Cultural Services, Augusta

Robert L. Hillerich, Ph.D., Bowling Green State University, Bowling Green, Ohio

CHILDRENS PRESS®
CHICAGO

Lobster traps, Boothbay

Project Editor: Joan Downing
Associate Editor: Shari Joffe
Design Director: Margrit Fiddle
Typesetting: Graphic Connections, Inc.
Engraving: Liberty Photoengraving

Library of Congress Cataloging-in-Publication Data

Harrington, Ty.
    America the beautiful. Maine / by Ty Harrington.
        p.   cm.
    Includes index.
    Summary: Introduces the state of jagged coastline,
mountains, lakes, and dramatic landscapes.
    ISBN 0-516-00465-4
    1. Maine — Juvenile literature.   [1. Maine.]
I. Title
F19.3.H37   1989   88-38399
974.1 — dc19   CIP
                                              AC

The rocky
coast of
Maine

TABLE OF CONTENTS

Chapter 1

IN PRAISE OF MAINE

IN PRAISE OF MAINE

Bloom-arbored, hundred-harbored,
Glorious state of Maine,
All the joys of nature
Lie in your domain.
   —Mildred Hobbs, 1924

Every morning in the United States begins in the state of Maine, where the nation's easternmost land is first graced by the dawn. Maine is a fitting place for the day to start, for nowhere else is democracy more firmly rooted in the soil. Nor is there a people anywhere more stalwart in their belief in freedom than those whose forefathers carved a new life from the hard rock and deep woods that characterize the state.

From the ancestors of the Indians who greeted the first Europeans, to the people who came to Maine from other parts of the globe, the taming of the wilderness has been a long, hard struggle. But simple living and hard work have always seen Mainers through, together with deep satisfaction in a job well done.

Ever since the early seafaring days, New Englanders have referred to Maine as Down East and Maine residents as Down Easters. This is probably because Maine lies east, and therefore downwind, of Boston.

As one of the New England states, Maine was a building block of the republic. In many ways it remains filled with the same spirit today. And in character and charm, whatever their origins, the people who live in the Pine Tree State reflect the values of the early Down East New Englanders of Maine.

Chapter 2
THE LAND

THE LAND

There it was, the State of Maine, which we had seen on the map, but not much like that—immeasurable forest for the sun to shine on, that eastern stuff we hear of in Massachusetts. No clearing, no house. It did not look as if a solitary traveler had cut so much as a walking stick there.
—Henry David Thoreau, 1846

Maine covers 33,215 square miles (86,027 square kilometers), making it nearly as large as the other five New England states combined. It is thirty-ninth in size among the fifty states. It stretches approximately 320 miles (515 kilometers) from north to south and 210 miles (338 kilometers) from east to west. The state is bordered by the Canadian provinces of Quebec and New Brunswick on the north and east, Quebec and the state of New Hampshire on the west, and the North Atlantic Ocean on the south.

Maine encompasses a rich variety of dramatic landscapes, ranging from a jagged, rocky coastline to a mountainous interior dotted everywhere with lakes. About one-half of the state's population lives within 20 miles (32 kilometers) of the coast, leaving vast sections of the interior so sparsely populated and undeveloped that it is still considered a wilderness. Nearly 90 percent of the land is covered by forests, adding an unspoiled character to the region. The state has three natural land regions: the Coastal Lowlands, the New England Upland, and the White/Longfellow Mountains.

Mount Desert is the largest of the thousands of offshore islands formed when the glaciers withdrew from Maine at the close of the Ice Age.

THE COASTAL LOWLANDS

At the close of the Ice Age, as the glaciers withdrew from North America about ten thousand years ago, the coastal land of Maine separated from the continent. It sank 1,000 to 1,500 feet (305 to 457 meters), forming an underwater continental shelf teeming with fish and other marine life. The peaks of these mountains remain today as Maine's thousands of offshore islands. Many islands are as much as 25 square miles (65 square kilometers) in area. The state's largest island, Mount Desert, has an area of about 100 square miles (259 square kilometers). At 1,530 feet (466 meters), Cadillac Mountain, on Mount Desert Island, is the highest point along the seaboard north of Rio de Janiero, Brazil. Although the coast of Maine is only 228 miles (367 kilometers) long as the crow flies, the actual craggy shoreline stretches 3,478 miles (5,597 kilometers), forming one of the most jigsawed shorelines in the world.

Potatoes and oats are among the most important crops that grow in the deep, fertile soil of the New England Upland.

The southern lowlands are characterized by sandy beaches and salt marshes. Old Orchard Beach, an 11-mile- (18-kilometer-) long swath of hard-packed sand, is one of the longest and smoothest beaches in the world. Farther north, the beaches are small sand strips nestled between high, rugged cliffs. The Coastal Lowlands extend 10 to 40 miles (16 to 64 kilometers) inland from the coast.

THE NEW ENGLAND UPLAND

North and west of the Coastal Lowlands lies the New England Upland. This is the predominant land region of Maine. In the south, the Upland stretches 20 miles (32 kilometers) across the state. In the more northern reaches of the state, the Upland may stretch as many as 50 miles (80 kilometers) westward from the lowlands. The Upland rises from sea level in the east to as much as 2,000 feet (610 meters) in the west. In the northeast, the Aroostook Plateau provides the deep, fertile soil that supports the state's potato crop.

Beautiful Mount Katahdin is Maine's highest mountain.

THE WHITE/LONGFELLOW MOUNTAINS

Maine's Longfellow Mountains are part of the White Mountain range, which is part of the Appalachian system. The mountain region is about 5 miles (8 kilometers) wide in the north and spreads to about 30 miles (48 kilometers) in the south.

A series of low gravel ridges called horsebacks, or kames, cover part of the mountain region, but by far the most spectacular features are the mountain peaks. Some of the highest peaks are Sugarloaf, Old Speck, Crocker, Saddleback, and Bigelow. In all, ninety-seven peaks loom over 3,000 feet (914 meters) high. Many give the impression that they are as high as the Rocky Mountains because they rise from near sea level, whereas the Rockies begin from a high plateau. Mount Katahdin, the state's highest peak, towers from its base near the shores of the West Branch of the Penobscot River to a cloud-splitting 5,267 feet (1,605 meters). Mainers with a sense of humor have erected a 13-foot (4-meter) tower on the top to make Mount Katahdin measure

More than two thousand lakes are scattered throughout Maine. Most of them were formed when the glaciers retreated from the area about ten thousand years ago.

exactly one mile high. The region has stirred the emotions of many travelers, including naturalist and philosopher Henry David Thoreau, who wrote: "Katahdin presented a different aspect from any mountain I have ever seen, there being a greater proportion of naked rock rising abruptly from the forest; and we looked up at this blue barrier as if it were some fragment of a wall which anciently bounded the earth in that direction."

LAKES AND RIVERS

Scattered throughout Maine, more than two thousand lakes cover more than 2,295 square miles (5,944 square kilometers). Moosehead Lake, which covers about 120 square miles (311 square kilometers), is one of the largest lakes in the nation that

The Penobscot (above) is among the more than five thousand rivers and streams that flow through Maine to the Atlantic Ocean. The city of Bangor is located on the Penobscot and the capital city of Augusta lies on the Kennebec.

lies within a single state. Most of the state's lakes, along with a great many waterfalls, were formed when the glaciers retreated from the land. Left behind were deposits of gravel, sand, and clay, which dammed the pre-glacial valleys. As the glacial ice melted, the valleys flooded. Because the glaciers moved through many high mountain passes, Maine has an abundance of lakes at high elevations.

Connecting the lakes and carrying the water down to the sea are more than five thousand rivers and streams. Ten of Maine's sixteen counties are accessible to water traffic. The Kennebec and Penobscot rivers rise in north-central Maine, wind through the state, and empty into the Atlantic Ocean. Other important rivers include the Androscoggin, the Saco, the St. Croix, and the St. John.

Most of Maine's land is covered with trees,
and the sparsely populated forests in the north
are home to many varieties of animals, including
moose (above), beavers, deer, and black bears.

PLANTS AND ANIMALS

Except for the Aroostook Plateau and a narrow swath along the
coast, Maine is carpeted by forests. All but 10 percent of the land
is covered with trees. The large number of towering pines,
spruces, and firs keeps the state green all year. Other trees
common to Maine are balsam, basswood, beech, hemlock, maple,
oak, and birch. The harvesting of these valuable trees employs
nearly one of every four people and has made Maine a leading
producer of pulp, paper, and lumber.

The sparsely populated forests are home to bobcats, black bears,
deer, moose, beavers, lynx, mink, and many other small animals.
Among the hundreds of varieties of flowering plants that grow in
Maine are black-eyed Susans, mayflowers, lady's slippers, clover,
goldenrod, sea lavender, Indian pipes, and anemones. Shrubs such
as alder, witch hazel, hawthorn, sumac, and chokeberry are also
found. East of Bangor, near Cherryfield, wild blueberry bushes,
with only a minimum amount of help from local farmers, grow so

Among the hundreds of varieties of flowering plants and shrubs that grow in Maine and the more than three hundred kinds of birds that make their home there are (clockwise from left) wild blueberries, Canada geese, herring gulls, lady's slippers, and goldenrod.

thickly that 20 million pounds (9 million kilograms) of blueberries are picked for market yearly.

More than 320 kinds of birds make their home in Maine, including Canada geese, ducks, teals, plovers, partridges, robins, chickadees, gulls, sparrows, swallows, and wrens.

Maine's lakes, rivers, and shores are home to many fish and shellfish. Freshwater fish include bass, trout, perch, and salmon. Cod, haddock, flounder, hake, mackerel, halibut, and tuna can be found off Maine's coasts. The coastal waters also yield oysters, clams, crabs, scallops, shrimp, mussels, and lobsters.

CLIMATE

"Drop the seeds in the ground, hoe 'em under, and jump back," is the way Maine farmers have long described the favorable planting conditions of their weather. And Mainers will go on to tell you that the weather is favorable and healthful for people, too—at least for those who don't mind at least three months a year of below-freezing temperatures. The word they use most often to describe their weather is "invigorating."

Actually, it is true that seeds sprout amazingly quickly. But the reason is that the bedrock, just below the thin layer of soil, holds the sun's heat, and the year-round humidity from the ocean adds enough moisture to create an almost greenhouse environment. The weather itself is far less cooperative.

Summers are rarely hot, and the temperature often drops suddenly when cold air blows in from the Arctic. Throughout the state, the average temperature from June to October is 62 degrees Fahrenheit (17 degrees Celsius). In summer, the north of Maine is only a few degrees cooler. In winter, Arctic air and Arctic Ocean currents limit the warming effects of the Gulf Stream. The average winter temperature is 20 degrees Fahrenheit (minus 7 degrees Celsius). During these months, northern Maine is generally several degrees cooler. The state's record low temperature of minus 48 degrees Fahrenheit (minus 44 degrees Celsius) was recorded in Van Buren on January 19, 1925. The record high temperature—105 degrees Fahrenheit (41 degrees Celsius)—was recorded in North Bridgton on July 10, 1911. The growing season is less than four months in the northwestern regions of the state but lasts six months along the coast.

The state receives an average of 40 inches (102 centimeters) of precipitation (rain, melted snow, and other forms of moisture).

Snow blankets the land during winter in northern Maine.

Along the coast, 70 inches (178 centimeters) of snow falls in an average season. About 100 inches (254 centimeters) falls in the interior. In fall, the fearsome "nor'easter" (northeaster) storms begin to howl with gale-force winds. The United States Weather Service reports that so many storm centers pass over Maine that it is located in a "zone of maximum cyclonic frequency." This means that the state is in the path of rains and winds that are among the most powerful anywhere.

"Outsiders" marvel at the rugged, rough-hewn topography of Maine and often can be heard to comment, "It's a great place to visit, but living there could be a lot of work." But to the Maine residents who live close to the land, it is the place where they have built the strength of character and individualism that are their pride.

Chapter 3
THE PEOPLE

THE PEOPLE

*[The Mainer is] a man of dry wit and shrewdness and of a
general intelligence which I had not looked for in the
backwoods. In fact, the deeper you penetrate into the woods,
the more intelligent, and in one sense, less countrified
you find the inhabitants; for always the pioneer has been
a traveler, and to some extent a man of the world.*
—Henry David Thoreau

The spirit and determination of Maine's people are legendary,
and the devastating floods of 1987 tested these traits. Ten of the
state's sixteen counties were ravaged by floods.

Forty-eight hours of rain had overwhelmed the river systems of
the entire region. More than 2,500 homes were washed completely
away. Many of those homes were more than two centuries old.
Four hundred businesses were also destroyed. Throughout Maine,
the people were very specific about the sort of help they needed or
would accept from the federal government.

A federal inspection team soon discovered why. Many families
they visited had large stores of home-preserved foods. Wood was
available for heat, and a few people were using windmills to
generate electricity. These Mainers were prepared to live as
independently as the pioneers had nearly three hundred years
ago. It was no wonder they faced the devastating floods with a
frontier spirit.

More than 96 percent
of the people who live
in Maine were born in
the United States.

POPULATION

According to the 1990 census, Maine had 1,227,928 residents. In
terms of population, the state ranks thirty-eighth in the country.
Between 1980 and 1990, the state's population grew at a rate of
9.2 percent. The population gain in the entire United States for the
same period was 9.8 percent. This means that Maine's population
is staying about the same in relation to the country as a whole.
Much of the population increase is due to the beauty of the land
and the relatively low cost of living, factors that have attracted
people planning to retire on a fixed income.

According to the 1980 census, 3.8 percent of Maine residents
were foreign-born. Canadian, German, British, Irish, and Italian
immigrants continue to settle in Maine. In addition, the
immigrant population includes many Asians and Pacific Islanders.

Mainers who were born in the United States claim a variety of
ancestors. Nearly 60 percent of the state's population is descended
from British settlers. The second-largest group is the Franco-

The Episcopalians represent one of the largest Protestant denominations in Maine. Shown here are St. Paul's Episcopal Church in Wiscasset (above) and St. Savior's Episcopal Church in Bar Harbor.

American population. Those who migrated from Quebec to work in the textile mills and paper mills are concentrated in Lewiston, Biddeford, Brunswick, Waterville, Augusta, Rumford, and Millinocket. Most Maine descendants of the Acadians, who fled Nova Scotia in the 1750s, live in Aroostook County.

The nonwhite population of Maine is less than 1 percent. Included are Hispanics, Native Americans, blacks, Asians, and Pacific Islanders.

RELIGION

Religious preferences within Maine reflect the primary ethnic groups. About one-fourth of the population is Roman Catholic. Large Protestant churches include the United Methodist, American Baptist, Episcopal, and United Church of Christ. The Jewish population is concentrated in the major cities. There has been a resurgence of traditional beliefs among the state's Native Americans.

POPULATION DISTRIBUTION

Maine has always been sparsely inhabited. Experts guess that there were perhaps three to five thousand Indians living in Maine when the first white explorers came. Indian villages were, for the most part, clustered along the coast and the major rivers. In the late 1700s and early 1800s, much of Maine remained uninhabited and most of the population was still concentrated along the coast and the major rivers. It is nearly the same today. More than 50 percent of the state is uninhabited, and nearly 50 percent of the population lives within 20 miles (32 kilometers) of the coast.

By far the largest number of people live in the southern quarter of the state. Major communities in this area are Portland, Lewiston, Auburn, Sanford, Brunswick, and Biddeford-Saco. One of every four people living in Maine lives in the Portland metropolitan area.

THE PASSAMAQUODDY AND THE PENOBSCOT

The Indian population of Maine belongs to two Algonquian tribes, the Passamaquoddy and the Penobscot. In the nineteenth century, the state set land aside in Indian Township and Pleasant Point as Passamaquoddy reservations. Land on Indian Island was reserved for the Penobscots.

In the 1970s, these two Indian groups brought suit against the state of Maine and the United States government. The Indians held that the treaties of the late 1700s and the early 1800s, which transferred their lands to the colony of Massachusetts, had not been properly ratified. They claimed that the Indian lands— amounting to two-thirds of the land area of Maine—were seized illegally. They were now seeking restitution. The case was settled

out of court when the United States government set up a
$27 million trust fund for the tribes and granted them money to
purchase 300,000 acres (121,407 hectares) of land. In return, the
Indians agreed to drop all land claims.

REGIONALISM

The sense of regional pride has long played an important role in
the lives of the people of Maine. The isolation of the state and its
history has given the people a strong common bond.

There were some early regional differences between the French-
speaking population in the north of the state and the majority
Anglo-Saxon population in the south. Today, the French-speaking
Mainers—9 percent of the population—are scattered throughout
the state.

After the Revolution, the British were a common enemy to
everyone in Maine. Through the Civil War, the Industrial
Revolution, and World Wars I and II, often despite great
differences in economic levels, the people of Maine identified first
with Maine, then with New England, and then with the nation.

PORTRAIT OF A MAINER

A visitor of today has only to cross the line into southern Maine
and stop to ask directions to realize that part of the state is a
region unto itself. The accent is unmistakable, as is the way the
people speak with a gentle humor and a tendency toward
understatement: "Excuse me, sir," asked the tourist of the Mainer
leaning on his hoe, "Where does this road go?"

"It don't go anywhere," came back the farmer's deliberately
slow-paced reply, "It just stays here."

Chapter 4

THE BEGINNING

THE BEGINNING

It is believed that early man migrated to Maine in search of a legendary land where the sun came from. It was about ten thousand years ago, and the Ice Age had finally ended.

RED PAINT AND OYSTER PEOPLES

The earliest Mainers were roving stone-age hunters who left graves filled with tools as evidence of their way of life. Because these people used a natural preservative, red ochre, to line graves, they are known as the Red Paint People. Many of the heavy stone tools are so unusual that early archaeologists were not even certain of their use. More than fifty graves have been discovered so far, but there is still a great deal to be uncovered about the Red Paint People, who were among the first people in North America.

There is evidence that a second prehistoric people lived in the region more than a thousand years after the disappearance of the Red Paint People. Huge mounds of oyster shells left behind by these people have led anthropologists to conclude that oysters were a mainstay of their diet. About four thousand years ago, these "Oyster People" began to use bows and arrows. During the summer, they fished along the coast, and in the winter they retreated to the shelter of the interior forests. They were probably the ancestors of the Indians who greeted the first colonists from

Europe. The largest oyster-shell mounds can still be seen at the Damariscotta Peninsula. A visit to the archaeological sites there is a fascinating introduction to a puzzle still waiting to be solved.

THE ALGONQUIANS

By the end of the sixteenth century, when Europeans began colonization, there were more than twenty Algonquian tribes in Maine. They called themselves *Wabanaki*, meaning "people of the dawn."

One of the major tribes in Maine was the Passamaquoddy, who lived in the easternmost regions of the state, where the uplands are dotted with lakes. Farther south, in the area where the Penobscot and Piscataquis rivers meet, the Penobscot had established villages. The Kennebec Indians occupied the Kennebec River Valley.

All of these people spoke dialects of the Algonquian language. The Passamaquoddy lived primarily by hunting, supplemented by some farming. The Penobscot had cleared lands for raising crops such as corn and beans. The Kennebec, too, lived in an area suitable for farming. It is likely that all took advantage of the maple orchards and that maple syrup supplemented their diet of fish, game, nuts, and berries.

The types of housing varied with the location and climate. In the far eastern region, the people lived in wigwams whose poles met at the top to form a cone shape. In other areas, Indian homes were round and had domelike roofs; these usually housed one or two families. No matter what the shape, the structures were made of bark and skins stretched over a pole frame. Furs covered the earthen floor.

Whether primarily hunters or farmers, the Indians of Maine

Maine's Algonquian Indians lived in round shelters with domelike roofs that were made of bark and skins stretched over a pole frame.

were affected by the European passion for fur. As fur trading increased, competition among the tribes increased. As tribes moved about their hunting areas, they often met. Sometimes they bartered; other times they battled.

By the mid-fourteenth century, the tribes of Maine were fighting with the Acadian Indians to the north. By the time the Pilgrims landed at Plymouth Rock, a great many warriors had died and the once-mighty Indian tribes had become severely weakened. In addition, the visitors from Europe brought many diseases to the New World. Chief among these diseases were smallpox and bubonic plague. More than 75 percent of the Indian population died of the diseases.

THE VISITORS

The first Europeans to sail across the North Atlantic Ocean were the Vikings, probably under the command of Leif Ericson, the son of Eric the Red. Between A.D. 700 and 1000, Viking ships made frequent trips between Greenland and the northern Atlantic seaboard, probably including the region of Maine. Little is known about the Vikings' travels. Perhaps their purpose was to gather wood for Greenland, which had none. It does seem, however, that the Vikings had little interest in settling the land.

In 1497, John Cabot sighted what was probably Newfoundland or Nova Scotia (left), though some historians still believe he reached the coast of Maine.

Five hundred years later, in 1497, John Cabot discovered what was probably Newfoundland or Nova Scotia, though some historians still believe he reached the coast of Maine. Cabot claimed the land for Great Britain and returned to Europe. Cabot's reports did not make the region sound enticing. In 1524, Giovanni da Verrazano, in the service of France, explored the New England coast. He is the first European of record to sight the coast of Maine. Verrazano claimed for France the region he had explored. This marked the beginning of more than 150 years of conflict between France and England in North America.

Few early reports about Maine were positive: there was no gold there, it was not the round-the-world route to the "spice" islands, and the weather was cold and harsh.

Most European explorers made trips ashore only to trade for furs with the Indians or to obtain supplies. Occasionally, deep-sea fishermen gathered on a Maine beach to salt their fish to preserve it for the months-long sail home. By 1580, North American furs had become extremely popular in Europe, and the British launched a series of expeditions to the northern coast of the

In 1524, Giovanni da Verrazano (left) became the first European of record to sight the coast of Maine. Samuel de Champlain (right) built a colony at the mouth of the St. Croix River in 1604.

continent. Explorer Sir Walter Raleigh, returning with a romantic report of the land of Maine, was the first to arouse the interest of the English public.

THE COLONISTS

European colonists began to arrive during the early 1600s. In 1604, French explorer Samuel de Champlain built a colony at the mouth of the St. Croix River, the river that forms the southern portion of the current boundary between Maine and New Brunswick, Canada. In 1606, England's King James I granted to the Plymouth Company rights to the Province of Maine. The company then financed a group of settlers who landed at present-day Phippsburg and established the Popham Colony in 1607.

The first European arrivals—explorers, adventurers, and entrepreneurs—saw the fur trade as a way of making money in the New World. But that way of life was contrary to the philosophy and aims of the settlers. Fur trading was a solitary profession. A trader could expect to travel many miles each day while setting and checking his traps. In addition, if the trader chose to bring the furs to Europe in person, a long trip was needed. In contrast, the settlers wished to settle down in a single place, farm the land, and raise families. Unfortunately, the poor soil of Maine proved difficult to master, and the first communities were unable to sustain themselves. The winter of 1607 was exceptionally harsh. Ice clogged the harbors and Arctic winds sometimes reached more than 100 miles (161 kilometers) an hour. The French settlement on the St. Croix River and the British community at Phippsburg were both abandoned after only one winter. The Popham Colony did build a ship, the *Virginia,* the first ship built by Englishmen on the northeast coast of what is now the United States.

MAINE BECOMES BRITISH

After initial attempts at settlement failed, the French remained primarily interested in fur trading. Meanwhile, the number of British settlers increased. French trappers began to compete with the British trappers, who at first worked for themselves, and later worked for the Hudson's Bay Company.

In 1639, Sir Ferdinando Gorges, who was governor of New England, received a charter from King Charles I to the Province of Maine. This was the territory between the Piscataquis and Kennebec rivers and extended 120 miles (193 km) north and south. The first known government representing the people of Maine was established by Sir Ferdinando's son, Thomas Gorges. The court, which had both judicial and legislative functions, met at Saco, near the present-day resort of Old Orchard Beach, in 1640. By then, the British settlements had a solid toehold in the region. The Pilgrims from Plymouth, Massachusetts, controlled the area of present-day Augusta, Maine, as well as permanent settlements on several of the offshore islands. The furs the Pilgrims gathered from Maine paid all of their debts to the New England Council, which loaned land to settlers, within ten years.

The Hunniwell House, built in Scarborough in 1684, has been restored.

More British colonists arrived every year and farms were carved from the dense forests. The fledgling settlements clung to the banks of the major rivers that provided transportation to the sea along Maine's southern coast. Permanent settlements grew rapidly in Saco, Biddeford, Portland, Scarborough, York, and Monhegan. Under a separate grant, a group of Germans built a thriving settlement at Waldoboro, named for their leader, Englishman Samuel Waldo.

Maine prospered under the Gorges family. The first sawmill was built in 1631, and lumber began to be exported to England. In fact, the masts and wood from Maine solved a shortage that had threatened to beach the British fleet.

The year 1675 marked the beginning of one hundred years of war between the colonists and the Indians of New England. Continued development became too expensive for the Gorges family, and in 1677 they sold to Massachusetts the rights to the Province of Maine.

The early settlers had to clear their land of rocks and trees before building houses and beginning to farm.

THE FRENCH AND INDIAN WARS

Throughout the years of colonization and settlement, the French maintained a much better relationship with the Indians than did the British. One reason was that the French, more interested in trading than in settlement, were less threatening to the Indians' homelands than were the British. French Jesuits were also successful in converting a majority of the Indians in Maine to Catholicism. Many Indians learned to speak French and many French could speak the Indians' languages.

Meanwhile, the British continued to antagonize the Indians. Settlers continued to clear forests for farms, destroying the Indians' hunting grounds in the process. Often during the first 150 years, a Maine town was attacked or a farm was burned. But the colonists always returned and started all over again.

In 1690, British Fort Loyal (above) fell to French and Indian forces.

The English responded to the raids by attacking the Indians. Often, however, the Indians the British attacked were not the ones who had committed the raid. During 1675, so many Maine towns were attacked that the British colonists were chased completely out of the Kennebec and Casco Bay areas.

The French, recognizing the strength of the Indians as allies, assisted them in their campaign against the British colonists. The situation worsened. Finally, in 1689, England declared war on France. The Indians and the French joined forces and drove the colonists south, even capturing the British Fort Loyal, on the site of present-day Portland.

The British tried to push the French back, but lacked the strength. Meanwhile, the colonists, mostly left to fight for themselves, fought valiantly. In one attack on the fort at Pemaquid, fifteen soldiers held off charge after charge by a force of five hundred French and Indians.

In 1690, Massachusetts tried to solidify control by organizing the provinces of Maine, New Hampshire, and Massachusetts into the Massachusetts Bay Colony. Maine was the largest district. The rest of New England was becoming prosperous, but Maine was still very much a frontier besieged by warfare. In fact, by the end of 1691, all but four of the English settlements in Maine had been abandoned. Part of the problem was finally solved in 1697, when the Province of Maine agreed to give up some of its claims in the far north to the French.

The people of Maine had come to make Maine their home, and with typical New England stubbornness meant to succeed in the face of difficult terrain, weather, and Indians. It was their intention to make the best of what they had and to move forward to join the tide of British commerce. By 1700, many settlers had returned and rebuilt their towns, only to be driven out again when Queen Anne's War broke out in 1703. It ended in 1713. For the next three decades, there were fewer battles and raids. Maine lands were once again attractive to settlers.

In 1743, there were twelve thousand residents in the Province of Maine and nearly fifty towns had been built, with almost all of the colonists clustered along the coast south of the Kennebec River.

Fighting between the British and French colonists broke out again in 1744. During what was called King George's War, New England soldiers led by William Pepperell of Kittery captured Louisbourg on Cape Breton Island. In 1748, when this war ended, each side was forced to give back what it had won.

Then in 1754, as the British sought to take over French claims in North America, the French and Indian War started. Most of the burden of the war was borne by the people of Maine, who contributed the majority of the soldiers. The conflict finally ended when the British captured the French-Canadian City of Quebec. France signed the 1763 Treaty of Paris, surrendering to England all claims to Maine, and indeed to most of North America.

Chapter 5

INDEPENDENCE AND STATEHOOD

INDEPENDENCE AND STATEHOOD

By the mid-1700s, Maine had become one of the colonies' foremost suppliers of fish and lumber. Then, when British maritime law required that all goods traveling between ports of the Empire had to travel in British-built ships, the New Englanders—and Mainers in particular—became shipbuilders. Maine had the largest supply of oak and pine, and shipbuilding became its biggest business.

SEPARATION FROM BRITAIN

England's treatment of the colonies had been restrictive since the early days when the first settlers were pressured to provide a profit to parent companies back in London. Beginning as far back as 1691, even the backwoodsmen were angered by unfair laws, such as the one that reserved all white pine trees more than twenty-four inches (sixty-one centimeters) in diameter for the king's use. Taxation without representation followed, and Mainers, along with the other New Englanders, were increasingly disgruntled. Mainers strongly opposed the Stamp Act and banded together to find alternatives to imported British goods. The "York Tea Party" took place in 1774, when local Mainers destroyed a supply of British tea stored at York. A majority of Maine's citizens supported the colonies' desire for independence from Great Britain.

Yet, because of Maine's long border with British-held Canada, and because of the residents' British heritage, many Mainers also retained a strong loyalty to the king of England.

When the colonies went to war to force a separation from Great Britain, the region of Maine found itself divided by its mixed loyalties. One thousand of the twenty-one thousand troops of the Continental Army at Valley Forge were from Maine. Altogether, more than six thousand Mainers served in the colonial armies. Some of the state's residents became "Loyalists," and joined a militia fighting for the king of England.

In 1775, Falmouth (now Portland) was almost completely destroyed by the British. And in 1779, because of the large Loyalist support in the area, the British met little resistance when they took over Castine, at the mouth of the Penobscot River. On learning of this, Massachusetts organized the Penobscot Expedition to force the British out of Castine. The expedition set out of Boston with more than forty ships loaded with cannon, troops, and supplies. Once at sea, the expedition encountered a violent storm that took several ships. Troops who did arrive at Castine suffered outbreaks of fever. Worst of all, the British had learned about the expedition and had sent for aid from Halifax and New York. Under the leadership of Captain Dudley Saltonstall, the colonists suffered a crushing defeat. Many ships were destroyed by British gunfire and the rest were scuttled by the Yankees so they would not be captured.

YANKEE INGENUITY

Despite geographical isolation and the fact that they were seriously outnumbered, the Maine patriots stood firm. They used ingenuity and daring to compensate for their lack of firepower.

When Edward Preble was only eighteen and in temporary command of a warship during the Revolutionary War, he captured a British ship in Penobscot Bay.

For example, the British Navy routinely stopped Maine vessels to take the young sailors and force them to fight for the king. In return, the clever colonists turned off the lanterns in the lighthouses that warned ships of dangerous shoals. Instead, they hung a lantern around a horse's neck and let the horse wander up and down the beach. Most local sailors knew the area well enough to navigate by moonlight; the Royal Navy sailors did not. Many of those who mistook the horse's lantern for the lighthouse ran into the rocks and sank.

The British blockaded the harbors and river deltas in an effort to stop transportation and communication. In response, Mainers improved the roads and bridges, began overland mail delivery, and started a stagecoach service. As more and more fishermen and other Maine sailors were put out of business by the British Navy, more and more became privateers. They designed and built special small vessels, capable of great speed and maneuverability. Led by seasoned captains, they attacked anything afloat that flew the British flag. In 1775, a small band of citizens from Machias rowed out into the harbor, where they attacked and captured the British cutter *Margaretta*. This encounter is considered the first naval battle of the Revolutionary War.

Maine's first great naval hero was Commodore Edward Preble, from Portland. Preble went to sea as a privateer when he was only

In 1804, Commodore Edward Preble, in the U.S. frigate *Constitution*, led an expedition against the Barbary pirates off the coast of Africa.

sixteen. At the age of eighteen, while in temporary command of a warship, he captured a British ship lying in the Penobscot River. After the Revolution, Preble secured his place in history by leading the United States Naval expedition against the Barbary pirates off the coast of Africa and stopping them from interfering with American shipping in the Mediterranean. Preble's flagship was the nation's most famous warship, the *Constitution*.

Maine's contributions to the war were not confined to naval matters. Maine regiments were conspicuous at Bunker Hill, Ticonderoga, Saratoga, and Valley Forge.

The Revolution finally came to an end in 1783, and the new republic, the United States of America, was born.

STATEHOOD

The years following the Revolution were prosperous for Maine. The shipbuilding industry grew as New England enterprises sought to replace the ships lost during the war. Furthermore, much of the Massachusetts fleet had been destroyed during the Penobscot expedition. Until the fleet was replaced, the Maine fleet handled nearly all the region's trading business.

The population increased, too. As a reward for service in the war, Massachusetts gave many soldiers grants of land in Maine. At times, the colony sold Maine lands to Massachusetts citizens. Two hundred years later, there would be questions raised about how Massachusetts had obtained the land from the Passamaquoddy and Penobscot Indians.

The people developed a regional sense of identity and loyalty. A movement began for separation from Massachusetts. When the federal government passed the Embargo Act of 1807, limiting trade with foreign countries, Maine's shipping suffered and many Mainers lost their jobs. In 1812, disagreements between England and the United States caused the two nations to go to war again. The British occupied Maine east of the Penobscot River. Fortunately, Maine was saved. During the occupation by the British, Maine requested help from Massachusetts, but none arrived. The United States' victory in the war fueled Maine's desire for separation.

Maine's constitution was ratified by Congress in 1820 and the state was accepted into the Union. Maine was considered a non-slave, or a "free," state as part of an agreement, known as the Missouri Compromise, that admitted Missouri as a slave state.

At the time of statehood, less than one-fourth of Maine was settled. However, the population already numbered a quarter of a million, two and a half times what it had been only forty years earlier at the end of the Revolution. Maine had expanded rapidly in the 1790s and early 1800s because of an influx from eastern New Hampshire, Massachusetts, and southern New England. Nearly two hundred new towns had been incorporated.

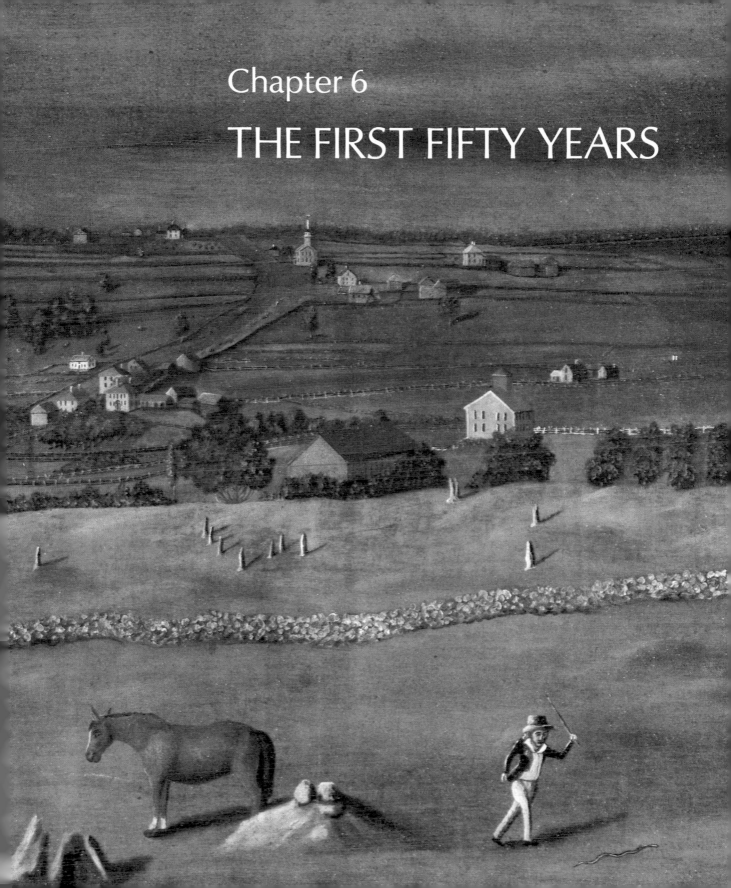

Chapter 6
THE FIRST FIFTY YEARS

THE FIRST FIFTY YEARS

Under the spreading chestnut tree
The village smithy stands;
The smith a mighty man is he
With large and sinewy hands.
And the muscles of his brawny arms
Are strong as iron bands.
—Henry Wadsworth Longfellow,
"The Village Smithy"

This poem is one of many describing the Maine life Longfellow recalled from his childhood. Community life centered on hard work, churches, and each other's homes. A favorite gathering was the quilting bee, where women of all ages would get together to make the large quilts used for warmth in the harsh winters. These were also social events that allowed the women and young girls of a community to exchange information, education, and gossip. They also offered an opportunity to be creative. Many of the elaborate, artistic, brightly colored quilts can still be seen in museums throughout New England.

Most homes were small cabins. Cedar shingles and other goods were used instead of money. Clothes were handmade, and during the week, work clothes were worn by everyone. But for church on weekends, and on special occasions, people dressed in crisp white and black clothes and, for some gentlemen, a red shirt.

Agriculture was developing. Potatoes, first brought to Maine in the 1700s by Scotch-Irish immigrants, had been added to the basic

During the early years of statehood, women would often gather at someone's home for a quilting bee, usually an occasion for as much gossip as work.

diet of fish or game and beans and corn. On their arrival, potatoes had been viewed with some suspicion, for they are not mentioned in the Bible. But the potatoes were well suited to the growing conditions in the Androscoggin, Kennebec, and Penobscot valleys, and by 1820 they were on their way to becoming the state's number-one crop. Nevertheless, Maine's economy—even the inland economy—was still tied to the sea.

In the early 1800s, Mainers continued their tradition of shipbuilding. The tradition had begun two centuries earlier, in 1608, when Mainers launched the *Virginia*. Between 1820 and the 1850s, Maine shipyards became famous for constructing some of the best cargo ships built anywhere. Lumbering, spurred by shipbuilding, quickly became the state's largest industry and remained so for a century.

In the 1800s, the harbors of Portland (above), Kittery, Yarmouth, Bath, Wiscasset, and Thomaston were filled with full-rigged sailing ships from all over the globe.

In Portland and the major harbors along the coast, there was a need for labor. Anyone who could handle a job was hired. The most flattering words that could be used to describe a person were *honest* and *hardworking*. The wharves of Portland, Kittery, Yarmouth, Bath, Wiscasset, and Thomaston were lined with full-rigged sailing ships from all over the globe. The crews brought knowledge from across the seven seas, lending a considerable amount of sophistication to the young state. Many Mainers signed aboard the cargo ships for voyages that often lasted several years. On their return, the tales of their adventures and of exotic lands fed the imaginations of others. Already known throughout Great Britain for shipbuilding, it was not long before the brave and hardy Down Easter sailors were legendary all over the world.

Many of the great wooden mansions built by wealthy ship captains and merchants during the eighteenth and nineteenth centuries survive today in towns such as Kennebunkport (left), Wiscasset, and Thomaston.

The area around Portland and the other harbors no longer looked like the frontier. Great mansions of Maine sea captains overlooked the forests of masts in the harbor. Many of these houses, usually painted white with black shutters, still stand today. Among the best examples are those in the Georgian style that still line High Street in Wiscasset and Main Street in Thomaston.

One of Maine's greatest strengths during the early 1800s was the opportunity for education. The Puritans' respect for education had prevailed. Schools were built even in the most sparsely populated regions of the state, though many had no more than one room. Bowdoin College had been founded in 1794 and Colby College in 1820. Even the children of the lighthouse keepers on the outer islands were able to go to school. Because of the emphasis placed on schooling, by 1900 Maine's standard of education was nearly as high as that in many more-prosperous parts of the country.

THE AROOSTOOK WAR

As Maine became more settled, colonists began to spread northward along the coast. In the northernmost regions of Maine, however, there was still a question of the boundary between Maine and Quebec. The Canadians claimed land as far south as Mars Hill, and the Mainers claimed an area that extended all the way to the St. Lawrence River. In 1838, Maine decided to secure its own land holdings and to grant land rights in the region to citizens of Maine. But Great Britain claimed that the northernmost lands belonged to the British Crown. The boundary that had been set by treaty in 1783 was the St. Croix River. However, the river had three branches and the treaty did not clearly specify the boundary branch.

Maine raised an army of 3,300 soldiers, and the United States Congress announced a war budget of $10 million. Tens of thousands of troops were made ready. Daniel Webster, the American secretary of state, and Lord Ashburton, a British envoy, effected a compromise before any battles took place. In 1842, the boundary at the St. John River in the north was agreed upon by both nations.

THE CIVIL WAR

Despite its geographical location, far removed from Mason and Dixon's Line, Maine played a very active role in events leading up to the Civil War. While their independent spirit may have led many Mainers to support the right of a state to secede from the Union, slavery was Maine's central issue in the Civil War. There were very few slaves in the region even in colonial times. Most of the black people in Maine were paid servants. In the 1780s, even

Harriet Beecher
Stowe at her home
in Brunswick, where
she wrote *Uncle
Tom's Cabin.*

before statehood, the Massachusetts constitution had granted to
all free citizens, including blacks, the right to vote. And after 1820,
admission of Maine as a free state under the Missouri
Compromise guaranteed freedom to all Maine citizens.

When the federal government passed the Fugitive Slave Law,
the issue became heated. The Fugitive Slave Law of 1850 required
that slaves who had escaped from slave states to free states be
captured and returned. As a result, free black men in Maine often
were accused of being runaways and were forced into slavery.
There were a few proslavery pockets of sympathy along the coast
because of trade with the South and the profitable use of Maine-
built vessels as slave ships. By the 1850s, however, the abolitionist
voice in Maine was strong. In 1852, attention centered on
Brunswick. There, Harriet Beecher Stowe, a minister's wife, had
written *Uncle Tom's Cabin.* The story, which graphically and
emotionally described the poor living conditions of American
slaves, became popular instantly.

Colonel Joshua Chamberlain's courageous Twentieth Maine Regiment
turned the tide for the Union at the Battle of Gettysburg.

The publication of *Uncle Tom's Cabin* greatly increased the anti-slavery sentiment throughout the northern states and made it impossible to enforce the unfair Fugitive Slave Law.

When war was declared, Maine sent approximately 70,000 soldiers to fight for the Union army. The Twentieth Maine Regiment was responsible for turning the Battle of Gettysburg into an important Union victory. The Regiment was given the responsibility of guarding the left side of the four-mile (six-kilometer) Union battle line. Suddenly, while Confederate General Robert E. Lee's main force was fiercely charging the front of the line, the Fourth Alabama Regiment charged the Maine soldiers from the side. The Maine troops were outnumbered two to one. When they were out of ammunition, they took out their bayonets and charged. The Confederate regiment, despite its greater strength, was so surprised by the boldness of the Mainers that it

These Civil War soldiers were members of the Portland Light Infantry.

retreated. The Maine regiment is credited with saving Washington, D.C. Its commander, Colonel Joshua Chamberlain, later was awarded the Congressional Medal of Honor. The First Maine Artillery Regiment, from the Penobscot Valley, suffered the heaviest losses. In an action at Petersburg in the summer of 1864, they left their cannon behind and charged forward on foot during the final push by Union General Ulysses S. Grant that ended the war with the defeat of Confederate General Lee. Of the 900 brave Mainers who fought there, 632 were killed or wounded.

The Civil War was costly for Maine. More than seven thousand died in service. The state had spent $7 million, and villages, towns, and individuals had raised $11 million for the war effort.

Chapter 7

THE EMERGENCE OF MAINE

THE EMERGENCE OF MAINE

*Think how stood the white-pine tree on the shore of Chesuncook,
its branches soughing with the four winds, and every individual
needle trembling in the sunlight—think how it stands with it now—
sold perchance to the New England Friction Match Company.*
— Henry David Thoreau, *The Maine Woods*

INDUSTRIALIZATION

During the Civil War, the introduction of metal ships powered by engines instead of the wind revolutionized the industry. Beginning in 1850, England took the lead in the production of steam engines, and shipbuilding declined in most of New England. Maine was an exception. Though many of the shipyards shut down, others remained in operation for years because the superior quality of their wooden ships was still in demand. Still others saw that much of the art of designing and building ships is similar whether the material is wood or metal. The Bath Iron Works and the Sewall Company of Bath began to build metal ships in the 1880s. Today, more than a century later, the Bath Iron Works is among the largest shipbuilders in the country.

Lumbering had relied greatly on the shipbuilders buying wood. Now it had to look elsewhere for a market. Fortunately, new uses for wood had been discovered. The most important to Maine was a process using wood pulp to make paper. The process required more than felling trees and cutting them into planks and boards. More powerful mills were needed to process the wood into fine pulp that could be pressed and rolled into paper.

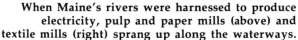
When Maine's rivers were harnessed to produce electricity, pulp and paper mills (above) and textile mills (right) sprang up along the waterways.

To solve the problem of additional power, rivers were harnessed to produce electricity. The cascading water produced an abundance of hydroelectric power. New pulp and paper mills, as well as other industries such as textile factories, began to grow in Maine. Businesses and the state competed for the best sites along Maine's swift-moving rivers. In 1909, the state acted to protect its interests. The legislature outlawed the sale or export of hydroelectric power to interests outside the state. In preserving the best power sites for Maine, the legislature hoped to attract new industries to the state.

Even farming began to industrialize. Instead of just growing a crop and sending it out of the state, farms and groups of farms began to operate their own processing plants. Small farms, particularly those in Aroostook County, soon gave way to larger, more-specialized farms that concentrated on potato crops and dairy and poultry products. By the early 1900s, Maine had become the potato capital of the eastern seaboard, and after World War II, it became one of the largest producers of chickens in the world.

The fifty-one Swedish settlers who came to Maine in 1870 built a town (above) still called New Sweden. For several years, the town hall (left) served as a church, schoolhouse, and gathering place. Within ten years, the population had grown to nearly eight hundred and the community had cultivated 20,000 acres (8,094 hectares) of farmland.

In addition, new sources of labor saw the developing state as a land of opportunity. A steady flow of Irish immigrants gave towns names such as Belfast, Connor, and New Limerick. French-speaking arrivals from France and from Canada went to work in the lumber and textile mills. Smaller groups of new arrivals came from other New England states, and invitations were sent to several special groups who would be able to make contributions to the economy. The most successful group was from Sweden. Invited by Maine to bring their expertise in farming to Aroostook County, they settled in what is today still called New Sweden.

The nationwide depression of 1890 was felt less in Maine than in many other states. One reason was that in addition to the post-Civil War influx of immigrants, Maine's industries and agriculture did not require large numbers of workers. So the westward expansion that weakened the labor pools of the more labor-intensive states had much less effect on Maine. In many ways, Maine entered the twentieth century in better shape than many of the more developed states.

INTO THE TWENTIETH CENTURY

By 1905, Maine's population had reached seven hundred thousand. Despite the more than four-fold increase during the past century, the state remained sparsely settled. The largest city, Portland, had seventy thousand residents. In comparison, the younger city of Chicago had already grown to three hundred thousand.

Along the coast, where Maine's commerce centered around the harbors, people lived moderately well. Though usually a year or more behind New York, many in Portland fancied the "latest" styles. In spring, they rushed to purchase items from mail-order catalogues in order to keep up with the wealthy New Englanders who spent their summers enjoying Maine's natural beauty.

In the south and far-north rural areas of Maine's interior, much of the population was poor. Because many had kept the pioneer ways of self-sufficiency, however, they were rarely lacking a warm home, good homespun clothes, and plenty to eat from their own gardens. Except during the years when the crops suffered from bad weather or insects, there was usually enough left over to barter for store-bought goods.

> How you gonna keep 'em down on the farm
> After they've seen Paree?
> How you gonna keep 'em away from Broadway?
> That's a mystery.

The words of the famous song, though sung with humor, told of the problems Maine faced following World War I. The 35,000 soldiers who left Maine to fight in Europe were restless when they came back. Many stayed home only long enough to visit before traveling again to seek their future in a big city or to head west.

Maine had spent more than $100 million to support the war, and the state treasury was depleted. This, coupled with the loss of its youthful work force, signaled the beginning of hard times throughout the state—a decade before the Great Depression swept through the rest of the country.

PROHIBITION AND DEPRESSION

Many people in Maine felt strongly about prohibiting the sale or consumption of alcoholic beverages. The Puritan ethic was in evidence again. To many people, Prohibition was what their ministers and priests meant when they spoke at church services about "clean living."

During the latter half of the 1800s, Maine was a leader of the Prohibition movement. Neal Dow, from Portland, was considered the Father of Prohibition. In 1846, Maine became one of the first states to outlaw the sale of alcoholic beverages. This law was difficult to enforce, however. Then, in 1851, the Maine legislature passed a more effective law, which banned the production and consumption of alcoholic beverages. In 1871, the Prohibition law was modified to include wines and ciders. Though Prohibition was strongly supported, individual freedoms were also highly prized by Mainers.

Many families in rural Maine had made their own liquor from apples for generations, and they continued to do so, law or no law. They felt it was their constitutional right to do as they pleased in their own homes. So long as they consumed what they produced, the police rarely disturbed them.

Nationwide Prohibition came into being with the Eighteenth Amendment to the Constitution. With it came the opportunity to make big profits with illegal alcohol. Many who faced Maine's increasingly hard times could not resist the temptation. The roar of fast cars, racing down the back roads of Maine with their headlights dimmed, told this side of the story. Maine's coastline and its long border with Canada made it a natural base for smuggling. As a result, from the 1920s until Prohibition was repealed in 1934, Maine was one of the foremost states for whiskey smuggling.

> Potatoes are cheaper, tomatoes are cheaper,
> now's the time to fall in love.

Despite the cheerfulness of this post-World War I song, Maine's economy failed to recover during the period following the war. The sudden widespread popularity of the Maine tradition of using potato starch to give clothes a crisp appearance provided a temporary boom, with Maine supplying 90 percent of the country's starch. But as the demand grew, so did the potato crops. Soon the market was virtually flooded, sending prices downward. By 1925, the potato farmers were unable to get enough money for their crops to pay their bills. The stock market crash of 1929 threw the state's economy into disarray, along with that of the rest of the nation.

MID-CENTURY MAINE

The middle of the twentieth century was dominated by World War II. As in the Civil War and World War I, Maine played a vital role in the nation's war effort. During a large part of the war, Casco Bay served as the base for the United States Navy's North Atlantic fleet. Thousands of sailors took their shore leave and spent their paychecks in Portland. Of even more importance to the Maine economy, the navy commissioned the shipyards to work full speed ahead.

Even though members of the Women's Christian Temperance Union were demonstrating against alcohol as early as 1910 (left), it was 1920 before national Prohibition went into effect. During Prohibition, some Mainers could not resist the temptation to profit from illegal alcohol. Smuggling (below) became big business, and liquor was hidden in such ingenious places as the false back of a record cabinet (above).

U.S.S. SPENCE DD512 PHOTO DOUGLAS
LAUNCHED 27 OCT. 1942
BATH IRON WORKS BUILDERS

U.S.S. CONY
LAUNCHED 16 AUG. 1942
BATH IRON WORKS BUILDERS

During World War II, the Bath Iron Works built dozens of destroyers, and even after the war, the shipbuilding company was busy around the clock.

The New England Shipbuilding Company of South Portland built more than two hundred Liberty ships, the Bath Iron Works built dozens of destroyers, and the Portsmouth Naval Shipyard (called by Mainers the Kittery Naval Yard) built more than seventy submarines. Welding torches burned day and night to speed victory, and the hundreds of vessels that were launched provided thousands of Mainers with jobs and a steady income. Ninety-three thousand Mainers served in the military during the war.

The end of World War II brought an era of prosperity and optimism to the United States. Everywhere the nation was building.

Maine lumber was again in great demand, both for new housing throughout New England and to feed the paper mills. Americans were suddenly hungry for millions of new books and scores of new magazines. Immediately following the war, the navy continued to keep the Bath Iron Works—and its workers—

busy three shifts a day. The postwar popularity of french fries and the perfection of the process for frozen potatoes, combined with new fertilizers and pesticides, brought prosperity to the agricultural communities.

Even so, there were factors working to weaken the state's economy. Just as small-scale farming had all but disappeared, many of the state's leather and textile mills moved to southern states where labor was less expensive. In response, the state moved to make Maine more attractive to industry. New laws provided tax incentives for businesses, and new highways were built. Construction workers were hired to build several air-force bases in the state. The bases also opened opportunities for businesses that provided services for base personnel.

In 1955, the State Department of Economic Development was established, as were a number of community-development groups. These groups, relying in part on the legislature's earlier incentives, continued to bring new business to Maine.

MAINERS IN GOVERNMENT

Although Maine is a relatively small state, with a total population less than that of many cities in the country, the state has produced a number of internationally known politicians. In the mid-twentieth century, Margaret Chase Smith dominated the state's political scene. A Republican, Smith was the first woman elected to represent Maine in the House of Representatives. She served there from 1940 to 1949. In 1949, she applied her energies to the United States Senate, where she served from 1949 to 1973. Smith's career was marked by hard work and dedication to the constituency that had elected her. Her Declaration of Conscience at the height of McCarthyism was a milestone.

As more and more New Englanders began to spend their summers along the coast of Maine, hotels such as this one on Monhegan Island were built to accommodate them.

In a move uncharacteristic for Maine, Edmund Muskie, a Democrat, was elected governor in 1955—the first Democrat to hold the post in nearly twenty years. Muskie went on to represent Maine in the United States Senate, and in 1968, he was the vice-presidential candidate. Later, he served as secretary of state under President Jimmy Carter.

George Herbert Walker Bush, inaugurated president of the United States in January 1989, has been a lifelong summer resident of Maine. Vice-president under Ronald Reagan from 1981 to 1989, Bush had also served as ambassador to the United Nations and director of the Central Intelligence Agency.

Senator George J. Mitchell, a Maine Democrat, began his duties as Senate Majority Leader at the same time Bush began his term as president.

VACATIONLAND INDUSTRY

After the Civil War, many wealthy New Englanders began to spend their summers along the coast of Maine. Bar Harbor was one of the early popular summer resorts. Soon, those seasonal vacationers were greeted by fancy hotels. They later built stately

When President Franklin Delano Roosevelt took a vacation home on Campobello Island, people across the nation became interested in Maine as a vacation area.

private mansions, which were called "cottages" in the Maine tradition of understatement.

Before World War II, President Franklin Delano Roosevelt took a vacation home on Canada's Campobello Island, just off the Maine coast. People across the nation learned of Maine's extraordinary beauty.

State of Mainers are quick to point out that Maine is not on the way to anywhere. Mainers are proud of their state and anxious to extend warm hospitality to visitors.

To accommodate the increasing numbers of visitors, many of whom were families traveling with children, the state government worked to improve tourist facilities. Hotels were renovated, and new motels were built along the highways. Hunting and fishing lodges opened in the woods farther off the beaten track. Today, Maine is a year-round resort region with fine ski areas. Though the state's economy continues to fluctuate, no one disputes the "Vacationland" claim on Maine's license plates.

The state is still nearly nine-tenths forest, and the coastline is largely unspoiled. However, Maine's future lies in its ability to balance the needs of the state's industries—both product and leisure-oriented—with its rugged, yet fragile, beauty.

Chapter 8

GOVERNMENT AND THE ECONOMY

GOVERNMENT AND THE ECONOMY

Maine was part of America's first frontier. In many ways, it is the nation's last frontier today. It is not a financially rich state, but its products are prized for being well made and there are no harder-working people anywhere. Business deals are straightforward, and are occasionally still sealed with only a handshake. Maine's heritage is in evidence everywhere, yet the state is poised for the future.

GOVERNMENT

Maine's government evolved along with the founding of the nation. Its constitution, based on the original constitution of Massachusetts, has not had a major revision since 1820. Like the federal government, Maine's government is divided into three branches: legislative (law making), executive (law enforcing), and judicial (law interpreting).

The state's legislative branch consists of a senate with 35 senators and a house of representatives with 151 representatives. Senators are elected to terms of two years. The terms are not staggered, so the senate may change completely in a single election. Members of the house also serve two-year terms. The legislature's responsibility is to create and to revise laws; it also has broad powers over the executive branch. Maine is one of only three states in which the legislature elects a council to work with

Blaine House, which now serves as the governor's mansion, was
the home of James Gillespie Blaine, a prominent Maine politician.

the governor. The legislative council has the right of approval
over nearly all actions taken by the executive branch.

The executive powers are held by the governor, the only
statewide official elected by popular vote. Elected to a four-year
term, the governor has the authority to veto or approve laws
passed by the legislature, to declare state emergencies, and to
appoint the officials in charge of more than twenty departments
and fifteen commissions. The governor may not serve more than
two consecutive terms, but may serve any number of terms. Other
members of the executive branch—the attorney general, secretary
of state, state treasurer, and state auditor—are elected by the
legislature.

The judicial branch interprets laws and tries cases. The Maine
court system consists of a supreme court, a superior court, and
district courts. The supreme court, the highest in the state, handles
cases that are passed to it from the superior and district courts.
The superior court hears all cases involving a jury trial.

TAXING AND SPENDING

Since the days of the colonies, finances and taxation have been dominant in Maine politics. Recently, the cost of state services has soared dramatically. The state income tax, first passed in 1969, and the general sales tax each provide about 40 percent of the state's revenue. In the late 1980s, the state budget rose to over $1 billion a year.

About 90 percent of Maine's general revenues are provided by taxes. Other taxes include those on fuel, alcoholic beverages, public utilities, tobacco products, insurance, and horse racing. There are also license fees and death and gift taxes. About 10 percent of the state's revenue comes from federal grants and other programs.

EDUCATION

During the 1980s, a large part of the total state revenue, particularly property taxes, was devoted to education. This represented an average cost of approximately $3,000 per year for each student. The state legislature provided a school fund in 1828, and tax support started in 1868.

The Indian mission founded in 1696 by Sebastian Rasle, a Roman Catholic priest, was probably the earliest Maine school. In 1701, a school for white children was opened at York. Many of the state's private schools are among the oldest and most prestigious in the nation. The majority of their students are drawn from throughout New England. Church-related schools are also important in the state's educational system. The Catholic French-Canadian communities help support the second-largest school system in Maine.

At the end of World War II, there were still several hundred one-room schools in use in Maine. Because of a statewide consolidation movement, only a few of these are left today.

Maine has fourteen accredited colleges and universities, including both public and private institutions. The oldest is Bowdoin College in Brunswick, which was founded in 1794. The largest school is the state-operated University of Maine, which began in 1865. The state university now has seven campuses with a total of more than 27,000 students. Among several specialty colleges are the Maine Maritime Academy at Castine and the Portland School of Art. Colby College in Waterville and Bangor Theological Seminary opened their doors in the early 1800s.

THE ECONOMY

Though the average income in Maine is below that of many of the more-populated states, so is the cost of living. This means that every dollar earned buys more in Maine. This fact makes the state attractive to business.

In addition to recent steady growth in its traditional industries, during the last half of the twentieth century Maine has experienced rapid development in a wide variety of new businesses, including those connected with tourism. During the past ten years, the state's most important economic indicator—the gross state product—has averaged a strong increase of 10 percent annually. The broadening of the state's economic base, coupled with the steady increase in development, paints an optimistic future for Maine.

While rare and valuable natural resources such as forests are the key to the state's economy, Maine will need to plan efficiently to both use and preserve these resources.

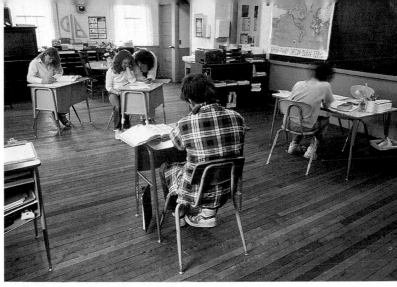

Schools in Maine include (clockwise from below) Bowdoin College in Brunswick; the University of Maine at Presque Isle; Bates College in Lewiston; the University of Southern Maine in Portland; Park School in Caribou; and one of the few multi-grade schools still in operation in the state.

Traditional and modern elements now share the waterfront area of Portland, where many nineteenth-century warehouses have been refurbished and new condominiums such as these have been built.

THE CITIES

Because the state's population is clustered in a few urban areas, each of Maine's larger cities plays a vital role in the state's economy. Foremost is Portland, by far the state's most-populated city. Surrounded on three sides by water, Portland was originally a center for shipbuilding and seaport activities. Today, it is the state's cultural and commercial center. Portland provides commercial services for southern Maine, has easy access to the Boston, Massachusetts, area, and is a center for the food-processing and wholesale paper and pulp industries. Portland remains a shipping center, although its traffic is much diminished. Throughout the city, the nineteenth-century warehouses and crisp new developments signify the tradition and the future of Portland.

The twin cities of Auburn and Lewiston, on either side of the Androscoggin River, form the second-largest metropolitan center in Maine. Auburn successfully combines agricultural trading and industry. It was a major shoe-manufacturing center. Lewiston is the center of the state's textile industry. Together, the two cities represent a considerable commercial and cultural resource.

Bangor, the state's third-largest population center, provides commercial services for northern Maine. Once a railroad center, it is still a trade and distribution center. An international airport is located at Bangor.

Augusta, the sixth-largest city in the state, is home to the state government and is central to the state's economic well-being.

INDUSTRY

Manufacturing is by far the largest contributor to Maine's economy. Led by the production of paper and paper products, more than 110,000 people are employed in manufacturing industries.

Maine's forests are vital to the state's largest industries. Much of the state's enormous harvest of timber winds up at the sophisticated, modern paper mills scattered throughout the state. It is impossible to reach the outskirts of mill towns such as Skowhegan, Millinocket, Jay, or Rumford without catching the strong, pungent scent of a mill. The state's more than fifty pulp and paper mills make Maine the second-largest paper maker in the country. The Great Northern Paper Company in Millinocket and East Millinocket is one of the nation's largest producers of newsprint.

Other leading industries include the manufacture of leather products, especially shoes, and the production of lumber and

Maine has a long history of producing lumber, pulpwood, and wood products.

wood products. Shoe factories scattered throughout the eastern section of the state employ more workers than any other single industry. Though lumber and pulpwood are important wood products, the state also produces boxes, canoes, Christmas trees, clothespins, tennis rackets, ice cream sticks, skis, splints, croquet sets, and more than 26 billion toothpicks a year.

Maine has developed an extensive food-processing industry. The leading food products are frozen blueberries, chicken, and french-fried potatoes. Maine is the nation's number-one packer of canned sardines, although that industry has declined greatly since World War II.

SERVICES

Service industries contribute more than two-thirds of the state's gross product. Trade, wholesale and retail, is Maine's largest service industry. Nearly 20 percent of the work force is employed by the state government, making it Maine's largest employer. Other service industries include insurance and real estate, transportation and communication, and public utilities.

Potatoes are one of the state's most important agricultural products.

AGRICULTURE

Although one-third of all New England farms are in Maine, agriculture provides only 2 percent of the state's gross product and employs less than 10 percent of the work force. Milk and eggs are the leading source of farm income. Most of the state's dairy farms are located in Androscoggin, Kennebec, Penobscot, Somerset, and Waldo counties. Broilers were once an important source of farm income, and many single farms had more than ten thousand chickens. Today, Maine chickens provide large quantities of fresh eggs for the New England market. Other livestock raised in the state include beef cattle, hogs, sheep, and turkeys.

Potatoes, the state's largest crop, provide Maine's second-largest income from farms. Maine is one of the nation's leading producers of potatoes, surpassed only by Idaho and Washington.

There are approximately 7,000 farms in Maine and they cover more than one million acres (.4 million hectares) of land. The average farm is about 200 acres (81 hectares). Many of the farms in Maine are family-owned and family-worked. In general, however, the

The Atlantic Ocean off the coast of Maine is one of the best fishing grounds in the world, and nearly every port along the coast has a lobster-fishing fleet. Maine lobsters, famous the world over for their taste, are as much a symbol of the state as the pine tree.

long tradition of the small farm has been gradually giving way to sophisticated agricultural industry. Aroostook County, where 90 percent of the potato crop is grown, leads the state in industrialized farming. However, the rugged terrain, the climate, and the thin fertility of the soil in the rest of Maine continue to prevent the implementation of large-scale farming.

FISHING

Harvesting seafood is Maine's oldest business. The Atlantic Ocean off the coast of Maine continues to be one of the best fishing grounds in the world. Maine is one of the leading states in the value of its seafood harvest. It is the nation's leader in lobstering, with more than 22 million pounds (10 million kilograms) of lobster sold annually. Maine lobsters are world-famous for their taste and quality. Virtually every port along the state's coast has its own fishing fleet.

ENERGY AND NATURAL RESOURCES

The powerful rivers that race to the sea from the high mountains in the interior are one of the state's great natural resources and one of its largest sources of energy. Because of the availability of hydroelectric power, Maine was one of the nation's first states to generate electricity, and it remains a major producer today. The majority of water-driven turbines are located on the Androscoggin, Kennebec, Penobscot, and Saco rivers. About 25 percent of the state's electricity is supplied by hydroelectric plants, 40 percent by oil-burning steam plants, and the remainder by the Maine Yankee Nuclear Plant in Wiscasset.

Many of Maine's natural resources are still undeveloped. These include deposits of copper in Aroostook County that are estimated to be very valuable. The bedrock has yielded a wealth of gemstones, and Maine is today one of the country's foremost sources of tourmaline, beryl, and garnets. To date, the most important in-ground resources have been stone and clay, and sand and gravel. Sand and gravel are mixed with cement and water to make concrete.

In fact, most of Maine's industry is based on natural resources, which also include the forests, the food from the sea, and the hundreds of natural harbors along the coast. During the past twenty-five years, the state has paid increasing attention to the preservation and management of these resources. Ecology and conservation are among the most important political issues across Maine.

TRANSPORTATION

Rivers and the ocean served as the major highways in colonial Maine. Stagecoach lines did not exist in the state until the early nineteenth century. Today, Maine has a road system that serves cities, towns, and villages. There are nearly 30,000 miles (48,279 kilometers) of roads. An interstate highway, I-95, covers the 310 miles (499 kilometers) between Houlton, near the Canadian Border, and Kittery, near the New Hampshire state line. The 100-mile (161-kilometer) Maine Turnpike connects York and Augusta.

Maine has about 1,500 miles (2,400 kilometers) of railroad track. The Bangor and Aroostook, Maine Central, and Canadian Pacific are the major railroads. Passenger service was abandoned in 1960, except for the Canadian Pacific's Via Rail service between Jackman and Vanceboro.

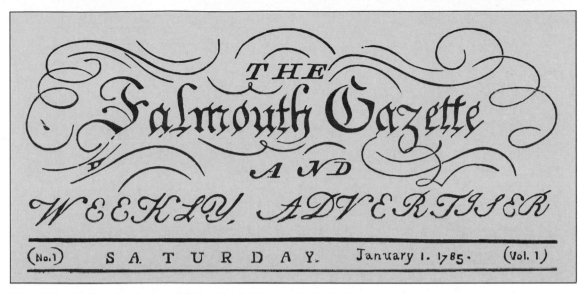

The *Falmouth Gazette*, first published in 1785, was Maine's first newspaper.

Because many of Maine's villages lie in rural areas, air travel is a popular mode of transportation. Maine has about 50 public and 110 private airports. Portland, Bangor, Lewiston-Auburn, Waterville, Bar Harbor, Presque Isle, and Rockland all have scheduled air service.

COMMUNICATION

Maine's first newspaper, the *Falmouth Gazette*, rolled off the presses in 1785. Since then, dozens of newspapers have circulated in the state. Today, there are about forty newspapers, eight of them dailies. Major newspapers include Augusta's *Kennebec Journal*, Portland's *Maine Sunday Telegram*, the *Portland Press Herald*, the *Evening Express*, the *Lewiston Daily Sun*, the *Morning Sentinel* of Waterville, and the *Bangor Daily News*, the largest.

Bangor was the pioneer city for Maine radio and television. WABI was the first radio station, in 1924, and WABI-TV was the first television station, in 1953. Maine now has about eighty-five radio stations and about ten television stations.

Chapter 9
CULTURE AND RECREATION

CULTURE AND RECREATION

In general, people in Maine don't believe in "things." They believe in sound thoughts and in deeds well done. For generations, many Maine households adhered to the rule: "Buy only what you can't make yourself." People in Maine made many goods by hand, with a bit of heart and soul thrown in. Fortunately, much of what they created over the years has survived. In the hand-built homes and the wooden ships, in the books and the poetry that have been written, and in the songs that have been sung across the seven seas, one can sense the character of the artists themselves. In their many works they have handed down a living legacy.

ARCHITECTURE

The first master builders in the New World were ships' carpenters who decided to stay ashore. They were expert woodworkers and they taught others. As a result, many of Maine's early buildings have endured two centuries of Maine winters and still stand today.

Some of the best examples of craftsmanship are found in the churches. Even the smallest of villages has one or more churches with tall wooden steeples. A close look reveals their simple elegance. Each piece of wood fits perfectly into the others. Because iron nails were scarce, many of the early buildings were constructed with only wooden pegs.

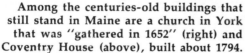

Among the centuries-old buildings that still stand in Maine are a church in York that was "gathered in 1652" (right) and Coventry House (above), built about 1794.

Clustered around the village green and in the older neighborhoods of the towns that have become cities, there are also centuries-old homes. Some date back as far as the 1600s. The earlier houses were plain and purposeful. An example is the "saltbox" design, which has a steep roof that allows snow to slide down safely to the back of the house. Another is the "garrison" design, with a second floor overhanging the first floor so that the occupants could keep a lookout or, if necessary, shoot at attackers.

Typical of the oldest homes are low ceilings and few windows, designed to keep in the heat. An excellent example is the Hunniwell House in Scarborough, built in 1684.

Wood was by far the most available, and hence the most popular, building material. However, brick and stone were also used. Maine had a large supply of top-grade granite, but most of it

This white wooden church in Farmington Falls, with its tall steeple and black shutters, is typical of many historic churches in Maine. The Longfellow House, built in 1785 (top right), is one of the oldest brick houses in Maine. The Moses Mason Mansion in Bethel (bottom right) was built in 1813, when the Federal style of architecture had become popular.

was shipped out of the state for construction of the nation's big cities to the south. The birthplace of American poet Henry Wadsworth Longfellow is one of the oldest brick houses in Maine that is still standing; it dates back to 1785. Granite was used for the majestic state capitol building in Augusta, erected in 1829.

By the beginning of the nineteenth century, the majority of homes and churches were being built in the larger, more spacious Georgian and Federal styles. They are characterized by higher ceilings, large windows, and usually several tall chimneys. Some of these dwellings were veritable mansions. Many of these old homes are open to the public. Two, kept as museums, are the

Victoria Mansion, in Portland, is one of the best examples
of Italian Victorian architecture in the United States.

Hamilton House (Georgian), built in South Berwick in 1787, and
the Moses Mason Mansion (Federal) in Bethel. In Farmington
Falls, the village's grand Federal-style church, with its typical
white sides and black shutters, is still in use.

The sea captains, returning with fortunes, were the first to build
majestic homes along the coast. Next to build were the successful
businessmen and merchants, many of whom were from outside
the state. The designs of the early "dream" houses were chosen
from the numerous styles popular throughout the world. Victoria
Mansion in Portland is still considered one of the best examples of
Italian Victorian architecture in the United States. It is elaborately
embellished outside, and inside there are carved wood decorations
and seven marble fireplaces.

85

Harriet Beecher Stowe (above) wrote *Uncle Tom's Cabin* in this house in Brunswick.

LITERATURE

From the earliest recorded history of the New World, the beauty and the freedom found in Maine have inspired the creative arts. There are few regions the size of Maine that have produced as large a volume of writings, poems, and paintings.

One of the most adventuresome visitors to Maine was Henry David Thoreau. Thoreau was an outspoken advocate of civil liberties and a keen observer of nature. His writings are among the first great truly American literature. Thoreau made three journeys to Maine from Massachusetts in the mid-1800s. He traveled overland by foot and up the rivers by canoe with a Penobscot Indian guide. In between these trips Thoreau wrote his most influential works, *Civil Disobedience* and *Walden Pond*. In *The Maine Woods*, he combined his philosophy with his expertise as a naturalist.

About the time Thoreau was traveling through the woods, a writer who was soon to help change the face of American society moved to the port of Brunswick. Harriet Beecher Stowe had been writing magazine stories to supplement her husband's small

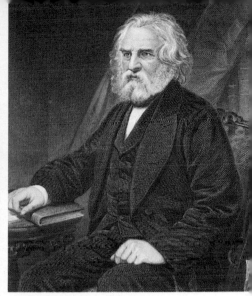

Among the most famous of Maine's many writers are (left to right) Kenneth Roberts, Robert Tristram Coffin, and Henry Wadsworth Longfellow.

income as a theology professor. Shortly after arriving in Brunswick, her sister sent her a letter that said, in part: "If I could use a pen as you can, I would write something that would make the whole nation feel what an accursed thing slavery is." Harriet Beecher Stowe rose to the challenge.

Uncle Tom's Cabin was meant to appear only as a short series of magazine articles. Instead, it became so popular that it was immediately made into a book. Three hundred thousand copies sold the first year in the United States, and millions more read it all over the world.

Poet Henry Wadsworth Longfellow, who wrote *The Song of Hiawatha* and other famous poems, was one of Maine's most gifted writers. He was the first American to have his statue placed in the poet's corner of Westminster Abbey, in London.

Sarah Orne Jewett, who lived all her life in South Berwick, captured the flavor of New England in her short stories and sketches.

Among the twentieth-century Pulitzer Prize-winning authors who were born in Maine are Kenneth Roberts and Robert Tristram Coffin. Novelist Kenneth Roberts is best known for

Maine has been a favorite subject for many artists,
including Frederick E. Church (*Otter Creek, Mt. Desert,* above);
Andrew Wyeth (*Northern Point, 1950,* right); Winslow Homer
(below left), who painted *Snap the Whip* (below right); and
Fitz Hugh Lane (*Owl's Head, Penobscot Bay, Maine,* bottom).

Northwest Passage, which has been kept alive by the classic movie based on the book. Robert Coffin based almost all of his many works—both fiction and poetry—on his love for Maine. Coffin won a Pulitzer Prize in 1936 for *Strange Holiness*. Popular poet Edna St. Vincent Millay received a Pulitzer Prize in 1923 for *The Harp Weaver and Other Poems*. Edwin Arlington Robinson won three Pulitzer Prizes in poetry during the 1920s.

In recent years, Maine has continued to be a home for writers. One of the nation's most popular gatherings is the Maine Writers' Conference held every summer in the coastal community of Ocean Park. Among the new generation just emerging is Carolyn Chute, whose novel *The Beans of Egypt, Maine*, about a Maine family living a rural life today, topped the best-seller list in 1985.

THE FINE ARTS

Several painters nurtured in Maine achieved international prominence. The most popular is Winslow Homer. Though Homer was born in Massachusetts, his parents were from Maine and he spent much of his boyhood there. In 1884, he made Prout's Neck his permanent home. Homer's dramatic seascapes capture the power of the forces of nature and the struggle of man against the elements. He found in Maine the weather and the subjects he needed for his masterpieces.

Critically acclaimed contemporary painter Andrew Wyeth has followed in Homer's brushstrokes. He uses many of the same subjects for works he paints during his summers in Cushing.

Maine has also produced a wealth of folk art. Hundreds of ships plowed through the waves led by a figurehead carved in Maine. The most successful figurehead woodcarver was Colonel C.A.L. Sampson, of Bath, who amassed a personal fortune from his work.

SPORTS

Today's professional sports teams are big business and require enormous amounts of money to operate. Even Maine's largest city, Portland, does not have a population large enough to support a major-league professional team. But that does not mean that Mainers have no sports loyalties. On the contrary, they are avid fans of the Maine Mariners hockey team. The Mariners are a farm team for the NHL's Boston Bruins.

In fact, because they are the closest team geographically to Maine, many of Boston's professional teams have been unofficially "adopted" by Mainers. Among the most widely-followed teams are the Celtics in basketball, the Red Sox in baseball, the Patriots in football, and the Bruins in hockey. Mainers are also extremely loyal to high-school and college teams, particularly football, basketball, baseball, and hockey. In 1993, the University of Maine won its first NCAA hockey championship, an event that caused excitement all over the state.

During the summer, Mainers are attracted to other amateur sports events, including sailboat and powerboat races. Even more popular are the individual sports practiced by serious outdoorsmen, experienced and novice alike. These personally-challenging sports include hunting, fishing, skiing, rock climbing, and water sports.

OUTDOOR RECREATION

Tourists have been traveling to Maine since the eighteenth century, when the state first became popular among outdoors enthusiasts, including people who love to hunt and fish. In 1840, Old Orchard Beach became Maine's first recognized resort area.

Maine has twenty-nine state parks, seven state wilderness areas,

Old Orchard Beach (above, about 1900, and right, today) has been attracting vacationers since 1840.

Favorite outdoor sports in Maine include fishing, canoeing, hiking, swimming, camping, sailing, skiing, white-water rafting, and even dogsled racing.

and five national parks and wildlife areas. These include the famous Allagash Wilderness Waterway, which provides canoeists, campers, and fishermen with 92 miles (148 kilometers) of rivers, lakes, and streams. Hiking, swimming, trail riding, camping, sailing, and just about every other outdoor activity are popular with both residents and visitors. Believed by the Indians to be the meeting place of the gods, Mt. Katahdin in Baxter State Park climbs to a spectacular 5,267 feet (1,605 meters) amid an expansive wilderness preserve. The popularity of winter sports has been steadily increasing since the first ski resort was built in the 1960s. Sugarloaf Mountain in Kingfield and Squaw Mountain in Greenville are favorite ski spots.

PERFORMING ARTS

A Yankee ship and a Yankee crew,
  Away now, rolling John.
A Yankee ship with a lot to do,
  Away now, haul away Joe.

Whenever groups of Mainers get together, there is music. In colonial times, with a great deal of physical work to be done, music made jobs easier. It was a sad ship indeed that did not have a chantey singer with a concertina or a harmonica to keep the pace and ease the chore of heaving up the great sails and the huge anchor. It was also the chantey man who played the humorous and romantic tunes the entire crew sang together for relaxation. A similar tradition of folk music grew around the campfires of the lumberjacks.

Maine has produced a number of band leaders, musicians, and composers. One of the first to achieve national recognition was military-march composer Robert Browne Hall, whose crisp compositions are still played by United States Navy musicians. During the twentieth century, Walter Piston—winner of two Pulitzer Prizes for orchestral music—has been among the nation's most popular composers.

Since the 1960s, there has been a revival of music throughout the state. There are symphony orchestras in Bangor and Portland.

Portland is particularly proud of its orchestra; a number of musicians from the prestigious Boston Symphony Orchestra also play for the Portland Symphony. Bowdoin College and the University of Maine also support symphony orchestras, and each college has a strong music department. The University of Maine String Music School is one of the best known in the country. The coastal towns and other summer communities present series of candlelight concerts during the summer months. Other concerts take place year-round, representing almost all types of music, including jazz, classical, folk, rock-and-roll, and country.

As with the other arts, Maine also attracts musicians from outside of the state. The first music festivals began in the 1920s, and today they are among the most popular cultural events in the state. One of the newest and brightest festivals is the Arcady Festival, which presents a full spectrum of works—from Baroque to contemporary—during the summer months.

Mainers are equally enthusiastic about theater. Though stage plays were banned by the Puritans until 1750, Maine soon made up for the deprivation. Summer-stock theater as well as amateur community playhouses have been well attended ever since. Among the most notable theater companies are the Acadia Repertory Theatre, which stages performances in Bangor during the winter and in Bar Harbor during the summer, and the Camden Shakespeare Company. The University of Maine was the first college in the country to offer a degree in theater, an innovative tradition that has continued with experimental theater and dance companies. Bangor's Maine State Ballet stages the most popular classical dance performances. For years, Lakewood was known as Broadway in Summer.

Though Maine is a sparsely settled state, it is rich in cultural and recreational activities.

Chapter 10

HIGHLIGHTS OF
THE PINE TREE STATE

HIGHLIGHTS OF THE PINE TREE STATE

If you ask a native what Maine is like, most likely you'll hear, "It's hard to say, you'll have to come take a look yourself." If the offer is accepted, the following are the sort of places and activities to which you would be introduced.

THE SOUTH COAST

Few coastlines in the world can rival the coast of Maine, either for its natural beauty or for the charm of its ports. Fullest enjoyment demands an approach by sea. Graceful two-masted schooners known as windjammers, with "cargos" of sightseers and vacationers, still sail briskly up and down the waters during the summer.

Ideally, a sailing tour would start off the coast of Kittery. This is where Maine begins, an hour's drive north of Boston, Massachusetts. The first dozen or so miles are crowded—the sea-lanes are filled with enormous freighters, tankers, and sleek grey naval vessels.

Soon the schooner approaches the large drydock of the Portsmouth Naval Shipyard. The blockhouse of Fort McClary, on Kittery Point, stands as a stalwart reminder of Maine's long frontier period. Several villages up the coast, at Cape Neddick, stands the Nubble Lighthouse. Built in 1879, it is typical of the lighthouses for which Maine has become famous.

FREEPORT
YARMOUTH
PORTLAND —CASCO BAY
BIDDEFORD
KENNEBUNKPORT
OGUNQUIT
KITTERY POINT

The charming village of
Kennebunkport, on the south
coast of Maine, is a popular
summer vacation spot.

Slowly the shore climbs until it towers 100 feet (30 meters)
above the sea at Bald Head Cliff. Below the cliff is the village of
Ogunquit, the Indian name for "beautiful place by the ocean."
Its sandy beach is one of the most popular in the state.

West of Ogunquit, about halfway between the coast and the
New Hampshire border, are the Berwicks — South Berwick, North
Berwick, and Old Berwick. South Berwick is the site of the state's
first sawmill. It is also the home of the carefully preserved Sarah
Orne Jewett Memorial, the clapboard house in which the famous
writer lived and worked. The Hussey Manufacturing Company in
North Berwick, an important maker of agricultural plows during
the nineteenth century, displays the earlier machines.

Several unspoiled white-sand beaches lie up the coast. The
famous village of Kennebunkport, with its colonial-town
atmosphere, is the summer home of former President George Bush.
For three seasons of the year the harbor is a forest of masts,
though today they are metal instead of the wooden spars of old.

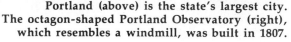
Portland (above) is the state's largest city.
The octagon-shaped Portland Observatory (right),
which resembles a windmill, was built in 1807.

The streets above are lined with rows of clean, white wooden
homes, with black shutters for protection from the northeast
storms that batter the entire coast in the winter. The Seashore
Trolley Museum, near Kennebunkport, houses the world's largest
collection of trolley cars. Nearby Kennebunk is home to what is
probably the area's most famous building, the elaborately
decorated Wedding Cake House, supposedly a gift from a sea
captain to his bride.

Out of Kennebunkport and around Cape Porpoise, the schooner
reaches the mouth of the Saco River and the commercial cities of
Biddeford and Saco. Nearby Old Orchard Beach is one of the finest
sand beaches in the world. This is the state's fastest-growing
region and the most popular for retirement living. Farther along
the coast is Scarborough, where artist Winslow Homer lived.

The next stop is Portland, the state's largest city and the center
of business and industry. Interesting sights include the home of
Henry Wadsworth Longfellow, the Portland Observatory, and the
ornate Victoria Mansion. Recent renovation of the waterfront area

The Old Port Exchange in Portland, a district of nineteenth-century buildings and warehouses that have been refurbished and converted to shops, theaters, restaurants, and pubs, attracts many visitors.

has resulted in the delightful Old Port Exchange, a district of shops, theaters, restaurants, and pubs that are housed in carefully restored nineteenth-century warehouses. The parks at either end of Portland offer spectacular vistas of the White Mountains to the west and the rocky islands of Casco Bay to the east.

Of the 136 islands in Casco Bay, Peaks Island is one of the most populated and can be reached from the mainland by ferry. The island was a favorite of the poet Longfellow, whose "Wreck of the Hesperus" was based on the 1869 wreck of the *Helen Eliza* on the offshore rocks.

On Cape Elizabeth, just south of Portland, is Portland Head Light. This famous lighthouse, built in 1791, is the oldest one in Maine, and is probably the most frequently photographed and painted lighthouse in the country.

Across Casco Bay is Yarmouth, which in the nineteenth century was a well-known shipbuilding town. Freeport, next door, is worth visiting if only because of the L.L. Bean store, which is open

The city of Bath (right) is the home of the Maine Maritime Museum, which displays many items related to the city's shipbuilding heritage and also offers an apprentice program (above).

twenty-four hours a day. The company has become one of the country's foremost outdoor-recreation outfitters, mainly because of its nationwide mail-order service. Because the incredible success of L.L. Bean has drawn a number of factory outlet stores to Freeport, the town has become one of Maine's most popular shopping districts.

THE CENTRAL COAST

Downeast of Casco Bay is a region of deep estuaries fed by several dozen rivers. It was here that lumbering and shipbuilding reached its heyday. The largest river is the Kennebec. Just a few miles inland on the Kennebec is the shipbuilding city of Bath. The Bath Iron Works, founded in 1889, produces United States Navy ships and merchant ships. The Maine Maritime Museum exhibits a fascinating array of historic items, including ship models, related to the town's shipbuilding heritage, which dates back to 1762. Bath is another port city that has refurbished its waterfront district.

Kennebec River Valley cities include Augusta, the capital; Waterville, home of Colby College; and Skowhegan, with its rich farmland. Augusta, on the banks of the Kennebec, has several sites of historic interest. The handsome capitol was built with granite from the nearby town of Hallowell. The State Cultural Building next door, which houses the State Library, State Museum, and State Archives, offers historical and educational exhibits. Fort Western, built in 1754 for protection against Indian raids, has been restored and now displays early military articles.

A short distance up the Androscoggin River is Brunswick, the home of Bowdoin College. The Bowdoin campus houses works by Maine artists Winslow Homer and Andrew Wyeth. Visitors to Brunswick may tour the Harriet Beecher Stowe House, where *Uncle Tom's Cabin* was written.

Heading back out to sea, the shore becomes increasingly rocky. Here and there are tall sand dunes. A little farther to the north are the villages of Boothbay and Wiscasset. Throughout this area there are dozens of museums, old forts, and lighthouses. In July, all of the windjammers in the state gather in Boothbay Harbor for a Windjammer Day that is reminiscent of the days when these swift, maneuverable vessels were manned by privateers battling

Pemaquid Point Light (right) is a
popular subject for artists and
photographers. The American art
collection at the Farnsworth Art
Museum in Rockland (above) includes
many Andrew Wyeth paintings.

the British. Farther up the coast, in the Damariscotta region, is the
Pemaquid Point Light, a popular Maine landmark.

The Lobster Festival is held the first week in August in
Rockland, Maine's largest fishing port. The town is also home to
the Farnsworth Art Museum, which houses an excellent collection
of Andrew Wyeth paintings. North of Rockland is the picturesque
village of Rockport. The old town hall in Rockport is now the
Maine Photographic Workshop. Rockport is one of the most
scenic spots on the coast, with the Camden Hills rising nearly
1,400 feet (427 meters) above Camden State Park in the distance.
The park offers some of the best hiking along the sea.

THE NORTHEAST COAST

The Penobscot River is the dividing line for the northeastern
region. In Hancock County, the ports—once haven to storm-
weary sailors—are now a summer haven for the city-weary. The
oldest of the exceptional homes in the area dates back to 1789,

During the summer, pleasure boats almost crowd out the working boats in the harbors of Mount Desert Island.

when the renowned British architect Christopher Wren designed the Blaisdell Homestead in Winterport. Farther downriver, Fort Knox overlooks the Penobscot. The fort was built from the same local granite that was quarried for the National Cathedral in Washington, D.C. Inland is Bangor, the commercial city for the region. Farther north is Old Town, well known for the beautifully crafted canoes made there, and for the several hundred Penobscot Indians who live on a reservation there.

Magnificent views of rugged Mount Desert Island can be seen while sailing up the coast past the fishing village of Stonington (on Deer Isle), and on through Blue Hill Bay and Frenchman Bay. Among the most spectacular spots in the nation is Acadia National Park. The park spans 22 square miles (57 square kilometers) of Mount Desert Island and Schoodic Point. It is an ideal place to explore by bicycle. The hardy might try the long climb to the summit of Cadillac Mountain, which affords the highest drop to the sea north of Rio de Janeiro, Brazil.

There is enough to do in Acadia National Park to fill an entire

The town of Machias, in "Sunrise Country," is the Washington County seat.

summer. Though the surrounding waters can be too cold for
swimming, visitors take advantage of the opportunity to
horseback ride, hike, camp, sail to surrounding islands for picnics,
and just enjoy nature. One beach in the park is composed of shells
so small that they feel as soft as sand to the feet. At Thunder Hole,
the crashing waves actually sound as loud as a thunderstorm. Bar
Harbor is the largest village in the area, and has dozens of
restaurants and plentiful lodging. Bar Harbor is crowded with
visitors from June until September. Nearly all the smaller fishing
villages in the surrounding area have quaint inns.

The long coast from Winter Harbor nearly to the Canadian
border is a feast of rugged, unspoiled beauty. Machias, site of the
first naval battle of the Revolution, has a campus of the University
of Maine. Nearby is a magnificent seaside park at Roque Bluffs.
Eastport, which claims to be the easternmost city of the United
States, borders the Canadian province of New Brunswick. Quoddy

Lush farmland in the Western Lakes region

Head State Park, just south of Lubec, is actually the easternmost point of land in the United States. A bridge at Lubec connects the mainland to Campobello Island. Though the island is owned by Canada, it has been a major American tourist attraction since the time President Franklin Delano Roosevelt made it his home.

THE INTERIOR

The interior of Maine can be visited by automobile, though much of the north country is accessible only by unpaved logging roads. A well-equipped four-wheel-drive vehicle is recommended for traveling through this area.

Aroostook is the northernmost county. Approximately one-fifth of the region is farmland, and just about all the rest of the area is a four-season outdoor recreational paradise.

The lakes and the fast-flowing streams lure fishermen from all over the country. Adventuresome travelers race down the world-

The Knife's Edge summit of Mount Katahdin (above) is the northernmost point of the Appalachian Trail. Eagle Lake (right) is in Aroostook County.

famous white-water rapids of the mighty Allagash River in rafts, canoes, and kayaks. Outfitters and Maine guides are available to assist visitors. The Aroostook Scenic Highway, Route 11, is lined with state-run picnic and camping grounds. As the road winds southward, it crosses into Penobscot and Piscataquis counties, which along with the western lakes and mountain region, rival the coast in spectacular natural wonders. Thousands of lakes and streams are surrounded by tall-timbered forests and hard-rock mountain tops.

Moosehead Lake, the largest lake in New England, is dotted with romantic islands and encircled by mountains. An excellent way to tour Moosehead is on the reconditioned S.S. *Katahdin,* built in 1914. At that time, before roads were built, "Kate" was used as a passenger boat to bring people and supplies to Mount Kineo.

Baxter State Park is the largest preserve in Maine. Towering over the park is Mount Katahdin, with its long, narrow summit called the Knife's Edge. Katahdin is the northernmost point of the Appalachian Trail. Baxter Park is an excellent place to see moose and a wide variety of other regional wildlife, including beavers and black bears.

Farther to the south, the inland sections of York County and the Kennebec Valley are more populous than the more-northern reaches, but they are also very beautiful, especially at apple-blossom time in the spring and when the leaves turn brilliant shades of red and orange in the autumn.

Museums throughout the interior give visitors a chance to step into the past. One of the most interesting is the Lumberman's Museum in Patten, a group of buildings that includes a replica of an early 1800s logging camp. Another favorite is the Norlands Living History Center in Livermore. Here visitors can put on nineteenth-century clothes and spend a few days getting a hands-on sense of what it was like to live and work in Maine during those early days. Willowbrook at Newfield Museum is a reconstructed village of colonial buildings that were moved there from throughout the northern interior.

After visiting some of these museums, it becomes even more noticeable how much of the past is still alive and well in the everyday life of the Pine Tree State. Only a few years ago, the village of Bryant Pond in the southwestern corner of the state was the last place in the nation still equipped with hand-cranked telephones.

From Kittery to Eastport to Bethel, nearly 90 percent of the state is still covered with forest. The frontier feels very much at the back door of every resident's home, and this living wilderness, combined with the ever-present remnants of colonial times, has kept a strong sense of history alive in the hearts and minds of the people of Maine. This gives them the same strength of character to meet the challenges of the future that their forefathers had when they first began to build the land that has become the United States of America.

FACTS AT A GLANCE

GENERAL INFORMATION

Statehood: March 15, 1820, twenty-third state

Origin of Name: Uncertain. Some believe it comes from the former French province of Maine. Most think it derives from "the main" or "mainland."

State Capital: Augusta

State Nickname: "Pine Tree State"

State Flag: Maine's state seal shows a farmer and seaman, depicting occupations of many state residents. A pine tree represents forests, and a moose represents wildlife. One lone star represents Maine's northern location. The word *Dirigo* ("I direct" or "I lead") appears above the drawing. Maine's flag, adopted in 1909, is a representation of the seal on a blue background.

State Motto: *Dirigo* ("I direct" or "I lead")

State Bird: Chickadee

State Flower: White pinecone and tassel

State Tree: White pine

State Fish: Landlocked salmon

State Insect: Honeybee

State Mineral: Tourmaline

State Song: "State of Maine Song," words and music by Roger Vinton Snow, adopted in 1937:

> Oh, Pine Tree State,
> Your woods, fields, and hills,
> Your lakes, streams, and rock-bound coast
> Will ever fill our hearts with thrills.
> And tho' we seek far and wide,
> Our search will be in vain
> To find a fairer spot on Earth
> Than Maine! Maine! Maine!

Twenty percent of the population lives in the Portland metropolitan area.

POPULATION

Population: 1,227,928, thirty-eighth among the states (1990 census)

Population Density: 36.9 people per sq. mi. (14.2 per km²)

Population Distribution: Although in size Maine is the largest of the New England states, much of the land is sparsely inhabited forest. About 48 percent of the state's population lives in urban areas, 20 percent in the Portland metropolitan area alone. Nearly half the population lives within 20 mi. (32 km) of the ocean.

Portland	64,358
Lewiston	39,757
Bangor	33,181
Auburn	24,309
South Portland	23,163
Augusta	21,325
Brunswick	20,906
Biddeford	20,710
Sanford	20,463

(Population figures according to 1990 census)

110

Population Growth: Maine's population growth has been slow for much of its history. Lack of high-paying jobs often forced young Mainers to move elsewhere. The forbidding winter climate kept outsiders from moving to the state. However, Maine experienced nearly the same population growth from 1980 to 1990 as the American average. Much of this growth can be attributed to the large number of Massachusetts and New Hampshire retirees who have moved to Maine's scenic coast.

Year	Population
1820	298,335
1840	501,793
1860	628,279
1880	648,936
1900	694,766
1920	768,014
1940	847,226
1950	913,774
1960	969,265
1970	993,722
1980	1,125,030
1990	1,227,928

GEOGRAPHY

Borders: Two Canadian provinces, Quebec and New Brunswick, border Maine on the east. New Hampshire and Quebec border Maine on the west. The Atlantic Ocean forms the southern border.

Highest Point: Mount Katahdin, 5,267 ft. (1,605 m)

Lowest Point: Sea level, at the Atlantic Ocean

Greatest Distances: North to south—320 mi. (515 km)
East to west—210 mi. (338 km)

Area: 33,215 sq. mi. (86,027 km²)

Rank in Area Among the States: Thirty-ninth

Rivers: A large system of rivers flows through the state, providing both transportation and hydroelectric power. The St. John River, Maine's longest, forms part of the state's northern boundary before flowing into the Canadian province of New Brunswick. The Piscataquis, at the southern end of Maine, forms part of the New Hampshire border. Other major rivers include the Penobscot, Kennebec, Androscoggin, and Saco.

Lakes: Glaciers advanced and retreated through present-day Maine for thousands of years. Their actions created hundreds of lakes. The two largest are Moosehead Lake, 120 sq. mi. (311 km²), and Sebago Lake, 44.8 sq. mi. (116 km²).

Views of the Maine coast have been favorite subjects of artists and photographers for more than 150 years. This painting, *Sunrise off the Maine Coast*, is one of Frederick Church's versions.

Coast: The coast of Maine from south to north is only about 228 mi. (367 km) as the crow flies. But if the crow followed every turn in the state's hundreds of coves and inlets, it would be a much longer trip. The coastline, counting offshore islands, is 3,478 mi. (5,597 km) long. Only Alaska and Florida have coastlines longer than Maine's.

Topography: Maine's topography can be divided into three distinct regions: the Coastal Lowlands, the New England Upland, and the White/Longfellow Mountains. The Coastal Lowlands extend only 10 to 20 mi. (16 to 64 km) inland, except for a wider stretch in the Penobscot Valley. The action of Ice Age glaciers formed the sandy beaches and rocky shores of the coast and the offshore islands. A hilly, transitional area comes between the coastal plain and mountains. This hilly region is 30 to 80 miles (48 to 129 km) wide.

West and north of the lowlands lies the New England Upland. This high, flat plateau—about 20 to 50 mi. (32 to 80 km) wide—extends into Quebec and New Brunswick. Most of the state's potato crop is grown along the eastern section of the upland. The western portion is heavily forested.

Mountains at the northern end of the Appalachian chain form the White/Longfellow Region. This part of the state contains nine peaks that tower more than 4,000 ft. (1,219 m) above sea level.

Climate: Many people treasure Maine's cool summers but dread its long, cold winters. Average summer temperatures range from 62° F. (17° C) in the northern interior to 65° F. (18° C) on the coast. Average winter temperatures vary from 18° F. (-8° C) in the north to 27° F. (-3° C) on the coast.

The "rockbound coast of Maine" often is a fogbound coast. Precipitation averages 45.7 in. (116 cm). Often precipitation takes the form of low-hanging clouds that cause heavy fog. The average rainfall in the potato land of Aroostook County is 40.2 inches (102 cm). The state's snowfall ranges from 70 in. (178 cm) along the coast to 100 in. (254 cm) in the interior.

Plants and flowers
that grow in Maine
include (clockwise
from left) cardinal
flowers, fireweed,
white pine trees,
red maple trees,
and blueberries.

NATURE

Trees: Forests cover nearly 90 percent of Maine and include balsam, fir, basswood, beech, hemlock, oak, maple, spruce, white and yellow birch, black willow, ash, and of course, pine trees.

Wild Plants: Hundreds of wildflowers add color to Maine fields and woods. A stroller may find mayflowers, lady's slippers, blueflags, white daisies, black-eyed Susans, clover, goldenrod, jack-in-the-pulpits, sea lavender, Canada lilies, trailing arbutus, buttercups, Indian pipes, orange and red hawkweeds, anemones, and harebells. Alder, witch hazel, hawthorn, shadbush, sumac, bittersweet, and chokeberry are among the shrubs that grow in Maine.

Animals: Maine's forests, lakes, and coasts are home to hundreds of different animals; among them are deer, black bears, bobcats, lynxes, beavers, otters, muskrats, minks, martens, weasels, skunks, rabbits, and porcupine. The majestic moose swims in the lakes and occasionally wanders near farms. The seacoast and open water also serve as home to many animals. Seals swim along the rocks. Sea mammals such as porpoises and even whales romp in the ocean.

Birds: Birdwatchers need not travel far in Maine to observe a wide variety of birds, including Canada geese, ducks, teals, plovers, partridges, robins, chickadees, bobolinks, jays, and orioles. Coastal residents and visitors may spot gulls, eider ducks, comorants, and puffins.

Fish: In the many rivers and lakes, freshwater anglers have a treasure of possible catches, such as bass, trout, pickerel, and landlocked salmon. Ocean fishermen try for cod, flounder, hake, mackerel, pollack, striped bass, tuna, haddock, and halibut. The shores also host shellfish such as clams, oysters, shrimp, and the famous Maine lobsters.

113

GOVERNMENT

Maine's government, like the people who formed it, has been solid and stable throughout the years. Mainers still use the same state constitution that they created for statehood in 1820. Based on the original constitution of Massachusetts, it has never had a major revision. There have been two Constitutional Review Commissions, one in the 1870s and the other in the 1960s.

Like the federal government, Maine's government is separated into three branches. The legislature consists of two branches, a senate with 35 members and a house of representatives with 151 members. Senators and representatives are elected to two-year terms. The legislators make laws and elect a council to serve with the governor.

Executive power rests with the governor, who is elected to a four-year term. The governor approves or vetoes laws passed by the legislature and appoints department and commission directors. The governor may serve any number of terms, but no more than two consecutive terms.

The judicial branch tries cases and interprets laws. Maine's court system consists of a supreme court, a superior court, and a district court. The supreme court has one chief justice and six associate justices. The fourteen-member superior court handles all cases involving trial by jury. Thirteen district courts handle cases involving damages less than $20,000. The governor appoints all supreme, superior, and district court judges to seven-year terms. Each county also has a probate court, whose judges are elected to four-year terms.

Number of Counties: 16

U.S. Representatives: 2

Electoral Votes: 4

EDUCATION

Maine, like other New England states, has always placed a high value on education. While there was little formal education available in colonial times, parents educated their children. Sometimes education was provided by the local minister. Today, children in villages and small towns attend consolidated schools. Those in larger towns and cities attend local schools.

Nearly 160,000 students attend public and private elementary schools. Another 70,000 attend secondary schools. Maine spends about $3,000 annually per student. A commissioner of education and cultural services and a nine-member board of education head Maine's public-school system. The governor appoints the commissioner, with legislative approval, to a four-year term. Board members also are appointed by the governor, with legislative approval, to five-year terms.

The Pine Tree State has fourteen accredited colleges and universities, both public and private. The University of Maine, a state-run school, now has seven campuses and more than 27,000 students. The school's largest campus is at Orono. Branches are located in Farmington, Fort Kent, Machias, Portland/Gorham, Augusta, and

Presque Isle. Other schools include the College of the Atlantic in Bar Harbor, Bangor Theological Seminary in Bangor, Bates College in Lewiston, Bowdoin College in Brunswick, Colby College in Waterville, Husson College in Bangor, Maine Maritime Academy in Castine, the University of New England in Biddeford, Portland School of Art in Portland, St. Joseph's College in North Windham, Thomas College in Waterville, Unity College in Unity, and Westbrook College in Portland.

ECONOMY AND INDUSTRY

Principal Products:
Agriculture: Eggs, milk and dairy products, broiler chickens, potatoes, apples, beef cattle, blueberries, cranberries, raspberries, sugar beets, oats, hay, maple syrup, hogs, lambs, sheep, turkeys, broccoli, dry beans, and peas
Manufacturing: Paper, leather goods, lumber and wood products, food products, textiles, hydroelectric power, electrical machinery, clothing, electronic products, shipbuilding, rubber and plastic products
Natural Resources: Quartz, feldspar, mica, graphite, asbestos, gemstones, granite, limestone, sand, gravel, brick clay, peat, perlite, lead, zinc, copper, and stone

Business and Trade: Ever since colonial days, the seaports and river ports of Maine have conducted active commerce. Portland and Bangor today are the most important commercial centers. The cities of Lewiston and Auburn are major textile-distribution centers. Searsport receives chemicals, coal, and oil for delivery to northern Maine. Portland also receives petroleum. Other major trade centers are the seaports of Bar Harbor, Bath, Bucksport, Eastport, and Rockland.

Maine's rural roads offer scenic views that aren't usually seen from the highways.

Finance: Boston, Massachusetts, financial hub of New England, also serves as the regional center of Maine. The entire state lies within Boston's district of the Federal Reserve System. Maine, however, has its own active financial system. The state has about 45 main-office banks with 486 branches. Maine also has about 15 savings and loans (with 22 branches), and 137 credit unions.

Communication: Maine's first newspaper, the *Falmouth Gazette*, rolled off the presses in 1785. Since then, dozens of newspapers have circulated in the state. Today there are about forty newspapers, eight of them dailies. Major newspapers include Augusta's *Kennebec Journal*, Portland's *Maine Sunday Telegram*, the *Portland Press Herald*, the *Evening Express*, the *Lewiston Daily Sun*, the *Morning Sentinel* of Waterville, and the *Bangor Daily News*, the largest.

Bangor was the pioneer city for Maine radio and television. WABI was the state's first radio station, in 1924, and WABI-TV was the first television station, in 1953. Maine now has about eighty-five radio stations and ten television stations.

Transportation: Rivers and the ocean served as the major highways in colonial Maine. Stagecoach lines did not exist in Maine until the early nineteenth century. Today, Maine has a road system that serves cities, towns, and villages. There are nearly 30,000 mi. (48,279 km) of roads. An interstate highway, I-95, covers the 310 mi. (499 km) between Houlton, near the Canadian border, and Kittery, near the New Hampshire state line. The 100-mi. (161-km) Maine Turnpike connects York and Augusta.

Maine has about 1,500 mi. (2,400 km) of railroad track. The Bangor and Aroostook, Maine Central, and Canadian Pacific are the major railroads. Passenger service is provided by Rail Canada.

Because many of Maine's villages lie in rural areas, air travel is a popular mode of transportation. Maine has about 50 public and 110 private airports. Portland, Bangor, Lewiston-Auburn, Waterville, Bar Harbor, Presque Isle, and Rockland all have scheduled air service.

The Portland Art Museum

SOCIAL AND CULTURAL LIFE

Museums: The pride Mainers feel in their colorful heritage shows in the many museums found throughout the Pine Tree State. Almost every small town has a historic house or a small museum devoted to the maritime past, the lumber industry, or the colonial days. The four buildings of Bath's Maine Maritime Museum include a working boatyard and exhibits of marine artifacts. The Grand Banks Schooner Museum in Boothbay is located aboard an authentic fishing schooner. The Penobscot Marine Museum in Searsport displays paintings, models, and objects brought by sailors from the Orient. Two museums, the Lumberman's Museum in Patten and the Ashland Logging Museum in Ashland, celebrate Maine's logging days.

Maine's scenery provides ample material for artists, and several art museums display local as well as outside talent. The Farnsworth Library and Art Museum in Rockland displays many paintings by famous Maine painter Andrew Wyeth, his father, N.C., and son, Jamie. The Portland Museum of Art has a collection of contemporary prints, nineteenth-century American paintings, and American decorative arts. The Walker Museum of Art at Bowdoin College in Brunswick has a collection that includes Old Masters as well as a large number of works by Andrew Wyeth and Winslow Homer.

The Seashore Trolley Museum in Arundel has the world's largest collection of streetcars.

Almost any subject may be the specialty of a Maine Museum. The Boothbay Harbor area has two of special interest. The Boothbay Railway Village, which features a collection of turn-of-the-century small-town shops and a miniature railroad, displays a large collection of antique railroad and automobile items. The Boothbay Theater Museum has portraits, engravings, sculptures, manuscripts, and other theater memorabilia that date back as far as the eighteenth century. The Seashore Trolley Museum in Arundel has the world's largest collection of streetcars. The Parson Fisher Memorial in Blue Hill displays paintings, wood engravings, and handmade furniture crafted by the town's longtime parson. The Maine State Museum in Augusta is a large historical and natural-history museum. The Maine Historical Society, in Portland, contains thousands of historical books and records.

Libraries: William Pepperrell established the first Maine library in 1751 at Kittery. The first public library appeared in Castine about one hundred years later (1855). Maine now supports about 175 public libraries. The largest ones are in Bangor and Portland. The state also has two notable research libraries, at the Maine Historical Society and the Maine State Library. The University of Maine and Bowdoin College also have important private libraries.

Performing Arts: Mainers like to think of themselves as doers, not watchers. Some of this "doing" takes place on stage. The Acadia Repertory Theatre offers performances on Mt. Pleasant Island in the summer and in Bangor in the winter. The Maine State Theater in Waterville offers a summer series of plays and musicals. Ogunquit and Monmouth have famous summer theaters.

Music lovers have enjoyed the Bangor and Portland symphony orchestras for more than eighty seasons. The New England Music Camp holds summer concerts at Oakland on Lake Messalonskee. Musical performances throughout the state feature jazz, classical, and rock music as well as the sea chanteys and other folk music well known throughout the country.

Bangor's Maine State Ballet offers classical and modern dance programs and opera can be enjoyed at the Bangor Opera House. Maine's colleges and universities also provide a full schedule of musical, dance, and dramatic performances.

Maine sports fanatics take advantage of a variety of available opportunities, including skiing, fishing (summer or winter), and sailing.

Sports and Recreation: Maine, because of its small population, has never attracted a major-league sports team. However, it has a top-level minor-league team. The Maine Mariners hockey team serves as a proving ground for future Boston Bruins stars.

Mainers nonetheless are sports fanatics. Winter's first strong ice brings out thousands of pairs of skates of would-be hockey stars. Others take to the slopes for some of New England's finest skiing.

The mild, yet invigorating, summer lures people for many different activities. Some enjoy boating or fishing off the coast. Others enjoy rock climbing, bicycling, trail riding, or camping in Maine's twenty-nine state parks, seven state wilderness areas, and five national parks and wildlife areas. Many energetic souls gather at Mt. Katahdin and start hiking. Maine's tallest mountain marks the beginning of the Appalachian Trail, a hiking trail that passes through eleven states between Maine and Georgia.

Burnham Tavern in Machias
was a meeting place for
American Revolution patriots.

Historic Sites and Landmarks:

Burnham Tavern, in Machias, was the site where townspeople planned the first naval battle of the Revolution.

Colonial Pemaquid Restoration, on the Pemaquid Peninsula, displays more than fourteen building restorations believed to be part of seventeenth-century colonial settlements, plus relics of earlier Indian habitation.

Eagle Island, off Harpwell, served as home to Colonel Robert E. Perry. His house contains memorabilia of the polar explorer.

First Parish Church, in Portland (Unitarian-Universalist), was the location of Maine's only constitutional convention, in 1819.

Fort Halifax, in Winslow, built in 1754, is believed to be the oldest blockhouse in the country. Benedict Arnold used it as a way station on his expedition to Quebec. Though it was entirely swept away in the flood of 1987, it has been reconstructed.

Fort Kent Blockhouse, originally built in 1838 for an anticipated border war with Canada, now houses a museum of lumber and Indian artifacts.

Old Gaol Museum in York is one of the oldest public buildings in North America.

Fort Popham, a granite fort built in 1861, is located on the site of several fortifications that have guarded the Kennebec River since the Revolution.

Katahdin Iron Works, in Brownville Junction, features restored ironworks from a nineteenth-century foundry.

Old Gaol, in York, built in 1720, is believed to be the oldest English public building in America.

Old German Church, in Waldoboro, built in 1772, contains boxed pews, a raised pulpit, and a church burial ground.

Old Harrington Meeting House, in Pemaquid, is a restored house, one of the earliest meetinghouses in Maine.

Pemaquid Lighthouse, on the Pemaquid Peninsula, is one of the most painted and photographed lighthouses in the United States.

Portland Head Light, on Cape Elizabeth near Portland, is one of the country's oldest and most well-known lighthouses. One of four lighthouses authorized by George Washington, it was built in 1791 and was the first put into service in the nation.

Tate House, in Portland's Stroudwater Village, is in a section of the city that was not burned during the Revolutionary War. Built in 1755 and since restored, it is the centerpiece of a site that includes original mills, canals, and homes that are more than 250 years old.

Willowbrook Restoration, in Newfield, a restored colonial village, conducts weaving, harness-making, and shoe-making demonstrations.

Artists painting the shoreline scene at Acadia National Park, Mount Desert Island

Other Interesting Places to Visit:

Acadia National Park, on Mt. Desert Island, is laced with scenic roadway and hiking trails. The top of Cadillac Mountain, accessible by road, provides a breathtaking view of the "rockbound coast of Maine."

Baxter State Park, in north-central Maine, is the largest wilderness preserve in the state and is the site of Mt. Katahdin, the state's highest peak.

Blaine House, in Augusta, once the home of prominent Maine politician James G. Blaine, now serves as the governor's mansion.

Colonel Black Mansion, in Ellsworth, has a formal garden and a carriage house filled with old carriages and sleighs.

Comsat Station, in Andover, is a communications satellite facility that offers guided tours.

Moosehorn National Wildlife Refuge, near Calais, provides a home for Maine's native animals. There are trails throughout the refuge, and visitors may view marsh waterfowl through an observation window.

Musical Wonder House, in Wiscasset, a restored Georgian house built in 1852, contains a working collection of antique mechanical music boxes and musical instruments.

Old Orchard Beach, near Kennebunkport, one of the finest sand beaches in the world, also has a boardwalk and an amusement park.

The Wedding Cake House in Kennebunk

Paul Bunyan Statue, located in Bass Park near Bangor Auditorium and Civic Center, honors the giant mythical lumberjack hero.

Rachel Carson National Wildlife Refuge, near Wells, named for the marine biologist and author, contains 4,000 acres (1,619 hectares) of marshland that is home to several species of birds.

Sandy River Railroad Park, in Phillips, offers rides on a narrow-gauge railroad.

State Capitol, in Augusta, is a majestic granite building that dates from 1829.

Victoria Mansion, in Portland, built in 1859, is an elaborate house that is considered one of the best examples of Italian Victorian architecture in the United States.

Wadsworth-Longfellow House, in Portland, preserves the memory of renowned New England poet Henry Wadsworth Longfellow. Built in 1875, it is the oldest brick house in Maine that is still standing.

Wedding Cake House, in Kennebunk, with elaborate outside decorations, was built by a sea captain for his bride.

Wild Gardens of Acadia, near Bar Harbor, displays more than two hundred native plants in nine distinct settings.

IMPORTANT DATES

8000 B.C. — First people, nomadic Stone Age hunters now known as the Red Paint People, enter land now known as Maine

3000-1000 B.C. — "Oyster People," hunters who left huge mounds of oyster shells, live in Maine

A.D. 700-1000 — Leif Ericson and other Viking explorers stop along the Maine coast but do not settle there

1580 — Sir Walter Raleigh reports to England's Queen Elizabeth about Maine

1606 — England's King James I grants the Plymouth Company rights to the Province of Maine

1607 — Mainers build the *Virginia,* the first ship built by Englishmen on the northeast coast of what is now the United States

1622 — The New England Council grants land between the Merrimac and Kennebec Rivers to Sir Ferdinando Gorges and Robert Mason

1631 — Settlers build first Maine sawmill and begin exporting wood

1675 — King Philip's War begins one hundred years of wars between English settlers and Indians, part of what is now called the French and Indian Wars

1690 — Massachusetts consolidates the provinces of Maine, New Hampshire, and Massachusetts into the Massachusetts Bay Colony

1719 — Scottish and Irish immigrants bring first potatoes to Maine

1763 — Massachusetts wins northern Maine and border territories from France as part of a treaty in the French and Indian Wars

1775 — Maine patriots capture the British armed schooner *Margaretta* in the first naval battle of the American Revolution; British burn Falmouth (Portland)

1782 — A treaty with the British sets the St. Croix River as Maine's northern boundary

1794 — Bowdoin College, Maine's first college, opens

1812 — War of 1812 begins

1814 — British occupy Maine east of the Penobscot River

1819 — Maine holds constitutional convention, voters overwhelmingly choose separation from Massachusetts

Hannibal Hamlin became vice-president of the United States when Abraham Lincoln was elected president.

HON. ABRAHAM LINCOLN, OF ILLINOIS.

FOR PRESIDENT.

HON. HANNIBAL HAMLIN, OF MAINE.

FOR VICE PRESIDENT.

1820—Maine enters the Union as the twenty-third state; becomes a nonslave state as part of the Missouri Compromise

1829—Mainers erect state capitol building, designed by Charles Bulfinch and enlarged in the early twentieth century

1833—Bath Iron Works opens

1842—A commission formed by the United States and Great Britain sets the St. Francis River as Maine's northern boundary

1851—Maine passes the first state Prohibition law, Neal Dow's Maine Law

1852—Harriet Beecher Stowe's book *Uncle Tom's Cabin* increases antislavery sentiment throughout northern states

1855—Bates College, New England's first coeducational institution of higher learning, opens

1858—Nathan Clifford, a former Maine congressman, is named to the United States Supreme Court

1860—Favorite son Hannibal Hamlin becomes vice-president when Republican Abraham Lincoln wins the presidency

1865—University of Maine opens

1884—James G. Blaine receives Republican presidential nomination but loses the election; Bath Iron Works builds its first iron ship

1911 — Maine adopts a direct-primary voting law

1923 — Maine native Edna St. Vincent Millay wins Pulitzer Prize in poetry

1936 — Maine and Vermont are only states to vote for Republican Alf Landon for president instead of Franklin Delano Roosevelt; Robert Tristram Coffin wins the Pulitzer Prize in poetry

1948 — Margaret Chase Smith becomes the first woman elected to the United States Senate; Walter Piston wins the Pulitzer Prize in music

1958 — Edmund Muskie becomes the first Democrat elected to the Senate by Maine voters since the 1910s

1961 — Walter Piston wins his second Pulitzer Prize in music

1969 — Maine passes its first state income tax

1972 — Penobscot and Passamaquoddy Indians file $300 million lawsuit over land claims

1974 — Nelson Rockefeller, born in Maine, is nominated by President Gerald Ford and confirmed by Congress as vice-president; James Longley becomes first Mainer to be elected governor without major party endorsement

1978 — E. B. White receives a special citation Pulitzer Prize for his writings

1980 — President Jimmy Carter appoints Edmund Muskie secretary of state

1989   George Bush takes office as president of the United States; George Mitchell becomes Senate Majority Leader

1993 — Youth Apprenticeship Program begins offering job training to young adults

IMPORTANT PEOPLE

Leon Leonwood (L.L.) Bean (1873-1967), born near Bethel; founded the nationally famous L.L. Bean outdoor goods store

John Bellamy (1836-1914), born in Kittery; artist known as one of the country's outstanding eagle carvers

James Gillespie Blaine (1830-1893), newspaper editor, politician; editor of Augusta's *Kennebec Journal* (1854-60); U.S. representative (1863-76), speaker (1869-75); U.S. senator (1876-81); U.S. secretary of state (1881, 1889-92); Republican presidential nominee (1884) who lost bitter election to Grover Cleveland

William Cranch Bond (1789-1859), born in Portland; astronomer; discovered the Great Comet of 1811 and the dark ring of Saturn

L.L. BEAN

CHARLES FERRAR BROWNE

GEORGE BUSH

MARY ELLEN CHASE

CYRUS H.K. CURTIS

Joseph Edward Brennan (1934-   ), born in Portland; lawyer, politician; governor (1979-1987)

Charles Ferrar Browne (1834-1867), born in Waterford; humorist who wrote under the name Artemis Ward; his letters from a fictional traveling salesman commented on general human weaknesses

George Herbert Walker Bush (1924-   ), forty-first president of the United States (1989-1993); lifelong summer resident of Maine; U.S. representative (1967-71); ambassador to the United Nations (1971-72); director, Central Intelligence Agency (1976-77); vice-president of the U.S. (1981-89)

Bill "Rough" Carrigan (1883-1969), born in Lewiston; professional baseball player; catcher for Boston Red Sox; manager of World Series champion Red Sox (1915, 1916)

Jean Vincent d'Abbadie, Baron de St. Castin (1652-1717), one of earliest European settlers; traded with Indians, protected Indian interests

Joshua Lawrence Chamberlain (1828-1914), born in Brewer; Civil War general, politician; governor (1867-71); president of Bowdoin College (1871-83)

Samuel de Champlain (1570?-1635), French explorer; built colony along mouth of the St. Croix River

Mary Ellen Chase (1887-1973), born in Blue Hill; author of books with New England themes; wrote *Dam in Lyonesse* and *Silas Crockett*

Carolyn Chute (1947-   ), born in Portland; author and columnist whose book *The Beans of Egypt, Maine* examined the state's poverty

Nathan Clifford (1803-1881), jurist; U.S. Supreme Court justice (1858-81)

Robert Tristram Coffin (1892-1955), poet and teacher; received the 1936 Pulitzer Prize in poetry for *Strange Holiness*

William Sebastian Cohen (1940-   ), born in Bangor; politician; U.S. representative (1973-79); U.S. senator (1979-   ); gained fame during Watergate hearings as thoughtful member of House Judiciary Committee; one of Senate's leading spokesmen on defense and military policy

John Wesley "Colby Jack" Coombs (1882-1957), professional baseball player; Colby College pitcher; as Philadephia Athletics pitcher, won 30 games plus 3 World Series games in 1910

Cyrus H.K. Curtis (1850-1933), born in Portland; publisher; founded Curtis Publishing Company, which published the *Saturday Evening Post, Ladies Home Journal,* and *Jack and Jill*

Dorothea Dix (1802-1887), born in Hampden; social reformer who worked for better conditions for the mentally ill

Fannie Harty Eckstrom (1865-1946), writer and Indian authority; wrote accurate, painstakingly researched books on Maine lumber camps and Indian life

Melville Weston Fuller (1833-1910), born in Augusta; jurist; chief justice of the United States (1888-1910)

Frank Bunker Gilbreth (1868-1924), born in Fairfield; efficiency expert who helped workers become more productive; his family was subject of the book and movie *Cheaper by the Dozen*

Sir Ferdinando Gorges (1566? 1647), English colonial proprietor of Maine

Hannibal Hamlin (1809-1881), born in Paris Hill; politician; U.S. representative (1843-47); U.S. senator (1848-57, 1857-61, 1869-81); governor (1857); vice-president of U.S. (1861-65)

Marsden Hartley (1877-1943), born in Lewiston; artist; best known for oil paintings of Maine landscapes, especially Mt. Katahdin

Winslow Homer (1836-1910), painter who spent much of his boyhood in Maine; best known for his magnificent seascapes

Oliver Otis Howard (1830-1909), born in Leeds; educator, Civil War general; Howard University founder (1867), president (1869-74); superintendent of United States Military Academy (1881-82)

Sarah Orne Jewett (1849-1909), born in South Berwick; author; known for her short stories of Maine seaports; wrote *Deephaven* and *The Country of the Pointed Firs*

Rockwell Kent (1882-1971), artist and author; worked for a time as a lobsterman and carpenter on the coast of Maine; wrote *Rockwellkentiana* and *It's Me, O Lord*; best known for his illustrations of literary classics

Rufus King (1755-1827), born in Scarborough; politician; member of Continental Congress (1784-87) and Constitutional Convention (1787); minister to Great Britain (1796-1803, 1825-26)

Stephen Edwin King (1947-   ), born in Portland; writer whose horror stories, such as *Carrie* and *The Shining*, became popular motion pictures

William King (1758-1852), leader in separation movement of Maine from Massachusetts; president of Maine's constitutional convention; first governor (1820-21)

Henry Wadsworth Longfellow (1807-1882), born in Portland; poet and author; best-known works include "Paul Revere's Ride," "The Village Blacksmith," *The Song of Hiawatha*, and *Evangeline*

Elijah Parish Lovejoy (1802-1837), born in Albion; abolitionist killed by a mob in St. Louis

John Marin (1872-1953), painter and etcher considered one of the most important American artists; gained renown for his paintings of Maine seashores

MELVILLE W. FULLER

FRANK B. GILBRETH

SARAH ORNE JEWETT

ROCKWELL KENT

HUDSON MAXIM

EDNA ST. VINCENT MILLAY

LILLIAN NORDICA

E.A. ROBINSON

Sir Hiram Stevens Maxim (1840-1916), born in Sangerville; inventor; mechanical genius who designed the first practical automatic machine gun; automatic sprinkling system, and electric current generator

Hudson Maxim (1853-1927), born in Orneville; inventor; brother of Sir Hiram Maxim; created an explosive more powerful than dynamite, a self-propelled torpedo, and a torpedo ram

John Rettie McKernan, Jr. (1948-   ), born in Bangor; politician; U.S. congressman (1983-87); governor (1987-95)

Edna St. Vincent Millay (1892-1950), born in Rockland; poet known for her New England images; her many volumes of poetry include *Renascence and Other Poems* (1917), *A Few Figs From Thistles* (1920), and *The Harp Weaver and Other Works,* for which she received the 1923 Pulitzer Prize in poetry

George John Mitchell (1933-   ), born in Waterville; lawyer, politician; U.S. senator (1980-1995); Senate Majority Leader (1989-1995)

Edmund Sixtus Muskie (1914-   ), born in Rumford; politician; governor (1955-59); U.S. senator (1959-80), first Democratic senator elected by Maine voters; U.S. secretary of state (1980-81)

Lillian Nordica (1857-1914), born in Farmington; operatic soprano; sang in London, Milan, Paris, Bayreuth, and St. Petersburg; member of Metropolitan Opera Association (1895-1909)

Sir William Pepperrell (1696-1759), born in Kittery; soldier; commanded New England's land force in successful attempt to capture French fortress of Louisbourg in 1745

Walter Piston (1894-1976), born in Rockland; composer; received Pulitzer Prizes in music in 1948 for *Symphony No. 3* and in 1961 for *Symphony No. 7*

Edward Preble (1761-1807), born in Falmouth (now Portland); U.S. naval officer; served in Revolutionary War and later commanded a squadron in the war against Tripoli

Thomas Brackett Reed (1839-1902), born in Portland; politician; U.S. congressman (1877-99); Speaker of the House (1889-91)

Kenneth Roberts (1885-1957), born in Kennebunkport; author; historical novelist who wrote such books as *Northwest Passage* and *Arundel;* received a special citation Pulitzer Prize for his historical novels in 1957

Edwin Arlington Robinson (1869-1935), born in Head Tide; poet, wrote "Richard Corey," "Miniver Cheevy"

Nelson Aldrich Rockefeller (1908-1979), born in Bar Harbor; politician; governor of New York (1959-73); vice-president of the U.S. (1974-77)

Margaret Chase Smith (1897-1995), born in Skowhegan; politician; U.S. senator (1949-73); first woman to seek a major party's nomination for the presidency (1964)

Samantha Smith (1972-1985), born in Augusta; Maine schoolgirl who became a symbol of worldwide cooperation when Soviet Premier Yuri Andropov invited her to visit Russia after she asked him for world peace

Seba Smith (1792-1868), born in Buckfield; editor, humorist, political satirist; poked fun at Maine politics and Andrew Jackson in the *Portland Courier*, which he founded (1829), and the *National Intelligencer*

Olympia Snowe (1947-   ), born in Augusta; politician; U.S. representative (1978-1995); U.S. senator (1995-   ); aggressive legislator

Bob Stanley (1954-   ), born in Portland; professional baseball player; relief pitcher with the Boston Red Sox; recorded more than 100 wins and 100 saves

Francis Edgar Stanley (1849-1918) and **Freelan Oscar Stanley** (1849-1940), born in Kingsfield; twin brother inventors who created the Stanley Steamer automobile and a plate-coating machine for photography

Harriet Beecher Stowe (1811-1896), author; while living in Brunswick wrote *Uncle Tom's Cabin* (1852), a book that exposed the cruel treatment of slaves and stirred antislavery sentiment in the North, and *The Pearl of Orr's Island* (1862), a novel with a Maine setting

Henry David Thoreau (1817-1862), author, civil-rights crusader, pacifist; gained fame for his quest of a simple life; wrote *Walden, Civil Disobedience,* and *The Maine Woods*

Giovanni da Verrazano (1485?-1528?), explorer; Italian sailing for France who was one of the first visitors to the Maine coast

Samuel Waldo (1695-1759), merchant officer in militia, colonizer of Waldo Patent, a large land grant including the site of Waldoboro; built lime mills in the area

George Weymouth (1507?-1613?), English explorer; sought Northwest Passage; explored Maine coast and described it in detail

Elwyn Brooks (E.B.) White (1899-1985), writer; considered one of America's best essayists; wrote "Notes and Comments" for *New Yorker* and "One Man's Meat" for *Harpers,* as well as children's books such as *Charlotte's Web* and *Stuart Little*

John Hay "Jock" Whitney (1904-1982), born in Ellsworth; publisher; published *New York Herald* and *International Herald-Tribune;* introduced Technicolor to movies

MARGARET CHASE SMITH

SAMANTHA SMITH

E.B. WHITE

JOHN HAY WHITNEY

ANDREW WYETH

Kate Douglas Wiggin (1856-1923), teacher and author; founded kindergartens; wrote children's books such as *Rebecca of Sunnybrook Farm*

Ben Ames Williams (1889-1953), author; summer resident of Maine; wrote more than 35 novels and 400 short stories, including *Evered* and *Immortal Longings*

Andrew Wyeth (1917-   ), artist; summer resident of Cushing; painter best known for his simple yet reflective landscapes

GOVERNORS

William King	1820-1821	Frederick Robie	1883-1887
William D. Williamson	1821	Joseph R. Bodwell	1887
Benjamin Ames	1821-1822	S.S. Marble	1887-1889
Albion K. Parris	1822-1827	Edwin C. Burleigh	1889-1893
Enoch Lincoln	1827-1829	Henry B. Cleaves	1893-1897
Nathan Cutler	1829-1830	Llewellyn Powers	1897-1901
Joshua Hall	1830	John Fremont Hill	1901-1905
Jonathan Hunton	1830-1831	William T. Cobb	1905-1909
Samuel E. Smith	1831-1834	Bert M. Fernald	1909-1911
Robert Dunlap	1834-1838	Frederick W. Plaisted	1911-1913
Edward Kent	1838-1839	William T. Haines	1913-1915
John Fairfield	1839-1841	Oakley C. Curtis	1915-1917
Edward Kent	1841-1842	Carl E. Millikin	1917-1921
John Fairfield	1842-1843	Federic H. Parkhurst	1921
Edward Kavanagh	1843-1844	Percival R. Baxter	1921-1925
Hugh J. Anderson	1844-1847	Ralph O. Brewster	1925-1929
John W. Dana	1847-1850	William Tudon Gardiner	1929-1933
John Hubbard	1850-1853	Louis J. Brann	1933-1937
William G. Crosby	1853-1855	Lewis O. Barrows	1937-1941
Anson P. Morrill	1855-1856	Sumner Sewell	1941-1945
Samuel Wells	1856-1857	Horace A. Hildreth	1945-1949
Hannibal Hamlin	1857	Frederick G. Payne	1949-1952
Joseph M. Williams	1857-1858	Burton M. Cross	1952-1955
Lot M. Morrill	1858-1861	Edmund S. Muskie	1955-1959
Israel Washburn, Jr.	1861-1863	Robert Haskell	1959
Abner Coburn	1863-1864	Clinton Clauson	1959
Samuel Cony	1864-1867	John Reed	1959-1967
Joshua L. Chamberlain	1867-1871	Kenneth M. Curtis	1967-1975
Sidney Perham	1871-1874	James B. Longley	1975-1979
Nelson Dingley, Jr.	1874-1876	Joseph E. Brennan	1979-1987
Seldon Connor	1876-1879	John R. McKernan, Jr.	1987-1995
Alonzo Garcelon	1879-1880	Angus King	1995-
Daniel F. Davis	1880-1881		
Harris M. Plaisted	1881-1883		

Topography

MAP KEY

Abbot Village	C3
Acadia National Park	D4
Alfred Mills	E2
Allagash (river)	B3;A3,4
Allagash Lake (lake)	B3
Alligator Lake (lake)	D4
Andover	D2
Androscoggin (river)	D1,2;E2,3;f7,8
Androscoggin Lake (lake)	D2
Aroostook (river)	B4,5
Atlantic Ocean (ocean)	E2,3,4;D4,5,6;g7,8
Attean Pond (lake)	C2
Auburn	D2;f7
Augusta	D3
Aziscoos Lake (lake)	C1,2;D1,2
Bailey Brook (brook)	B2,3
Baker Lake (lake)	B3
Baker Mountain (mountain)	C3
Bangor	D4
Bar Harbor	D4
Baskahegan Lake (lake)	C5
Bath	E3;g8
Beau Lake (lake)	A3
Belfast	D3,4
Berwick	E2
Bethel	D2
Biddeford	E2;g7
Big Indian Lake (lake)	D3
Big Spencer Mountain (mountain)	C3
Big Squaw Mountain (mountain)	C3
Bigelow Mountain (mountain)	C2
Black (river)	B3
Black Pond (lake)	B3
Boothbay	E3
Boothbay Harbor	E3
Boundary Bald Mountain (mountain)	C2
Boyd Lake (lake)	C4
Branch Lake (lake)	D4
Brassau Lake (lake)	C3
Brewer	D4
Brunswick	E3;g8
Brunswick Naval Air Station	E3;g8
Bryant Pond	D2
Bucksport	D4
Cadillac Mountain (mountain)	D4
Calais	C5
Camden	D3
Canada Falls Deadwater (lake)	C2
Cape Elizabeth	E2;g7
Cape Neddick	E2
Cape Porpoise	E2
Caribou	B4
Caribou Lake (lake)	C3
Caribou Mountain (mountain)	C2
Casco	D2
Casco Bay (bay)	E2,3;g7
Castine	D4
Cathance Lake (lake)	D5
Caucomgomoc Lake (lake)	B3
Chamberlain Lake (lake)	B3
Chebeague Island	E2;g7
Chelsea	D3
Chemquasabmticook Lake (lake)	B3
Chesuncook Lake (lake)	C3
China	D3
China Lake (lake)	D3
Chiputneticook Lakes (lakes)	C5
Churchill Lake (lake)	B3
Cliff Island (island)	g7
Cobbosseeconted Lake (lake)	D3
Coburn Mountain (mountain)	C2
Cold Stream Pond (lake)	C4
Connors	A4
Crawford Lake (lake)	C5
Cross Island (island)	D5
Cross Lake (lake)	A4
Damariscotta Lake (lake)	D3
Dead River (river)	C2
Dead River, North Branch (river)	C2
Dead River, South Branch (river)	C2
Debouillie Mountain (mountain)	B4
Deer Isle (island)	D4
Deer Mountain (mountain)	C2
Dexter	C3
Dover-Foxcroft	C3
Dow Air Force Base	D4
Duck Lake (lake)	C4
Durham	g7
Eagle Lake	A4
Eagle Lake	B3
East Dixmont	D3
East Dover	C3
East Millinocket	C4

Eastport	D6
Echo Lake (lake)	D3
Elephant Mountain (mountain)	D2
Eliot	E2
Ellis Pond (lake)	D2
Ellsworth	D4
Embden Pond (lake)	D4
Endless Lake (lake)	C4
Fairfield	D3
Falmouth	E2;g7
Farmingdale	D3
Farmington	D2
First Roach Pond (lake)	C3
Fish (river)	A4
Fish River Lake (lake)	B4
Fort Fairfield	B5
Fort Kent	A4
Freeport	E2;g7
Frenchman Bay (bay)	D4,5
Gardiner	D3
Gardner Lake (lake)	D5
Glazier Lake (lake)	A3
Gorham	E2;g7
Graham Lake (lake)	D4
Grand Falls Lake (lake)	C5
Grand Lake (lake)	B4
Grand Lake (lake)	C5
Grand Lake Seboeis (lake)	B4
Grand Manan Channel (channel)	D5,6
Gray	E1,2
Great East Lake (lake)	E2
Great Moose Lake (lake)	D3
Great Pond (lake)	D3
Great Wass Island (island)	D5
Green Lake (lake)	D4
Greene	D2
Hadley Lake (lake)	D5
Hallowell	D3
Hancock Pond (lake)	E2
Harrington Lake (lake)	C3
Haymock Lake (lake)	B3
Head Harbor Island (island)	D5
Highland Lake (lake)	g7
Houlton	B5
Hudson Mountain (mountain)	B3
Indian Pond (lake)	B3
Indian Pond (lake)	C3
Isle au Haut (island)	D4
Jackson Mountain (mountain)	D2
Jay	D2
Junior Lake (lake)	C4
Kelly Brook Mountain (mountain)	A3
Kennebago Lake (lake)	C2
Kennebec (river)	C,D,E3
Kennebunk	E2
Kennebunkport	E2
Kezar Lake (lake)	D2
Kezar Pond (lake)	D2
Kittery	E2
Lake Onawa (lake)	C3
Lake Wassookeag (lake)	C3
Lake Webb (lake)	D2
Lead Mountain (mountain)	D4
Lead Mountain Ponds (lakes)	D4,5
Lewiston	D2;f7
Limington	E2
Lisbon	D2;f7
Lisbon Falls	D,E2;f,g7
Little Black (river)	A3
Little Sébago Lake (lake)	g7
Livermore	D2
Livermore Falls	D2
Lobster Lake (lake)	C3
Long Island (island)	D4
Long Island (island)	g7
Long Lake (lake)	A4
Long Lake (lake)	D2
Long Pond (lake)	C2
Long Pond (lake)	C3
Loon Lake (lake)	C2
Loring Air Force Base	B5
Lovewell Pond (lake)	D,E2
Lubec	D6
Machias	D5
Machias (river)	C,D5
Machias (river)	B4
Machias Bay (bay)	D5
Machias Lakes (lakes)	C4,5
Madawaska	A4
Madawaska Lake (lake)	A4
Madison	D3
Mahoosuc Range (mountain range)	D1,2
Mars Hill (hill)	B5

Matinicus Isle (island)	E4
Mattamiscontis Lake (lake)	C4
Mattawamkeag Lake (lake)	B,C4
Mattawamkeag River (river)	C4,5
Mattawamkeag River, East Branch	B,C,4,5
Mattawamkeag River, West Branch (river)	C4
McLean Mountain (mountain)	A4
Mechanic Falls	D2
Meddybemps Lake (lake)	C5
Meduxnekeag River, North Branch	B4,5
Messalonskee Lake (lake)	D3
Mexico	D2
Millinocket	C4
Millinocket (lake)	B4
Millinocket Lake (lake)	C4
Milo	C4
Molasses Pond (lake)	D4
Monhegan Island (island)	E3
Monmouth	D2
Moosehead Lake (lake)	C3
Mooseleuk Stream (stream)	B4
Mooselookmeguntic Lake (lake)	D2
Mopang Lakes (lakes)	D4,5
Mount Blue (mountain)	D2
Mount Chase (mountain)	B4
Mount Desert Island (island)	D4
Mount Katahdin (mountain)	C4
Mount Kineo (mountain)	C3
Mount Megunticook (mountain)	D3
Moxie Pond (lake)	C3
Mud Lake (lake)	A4
Munsungan lake (lake)	B3,4
Musquacook Lake (lake)	B3
Musquash Mountain (mountain)	C5
Nahmakanta Lake (lake)	C3
Narraguagus (river)	D4,5
Nequassett	E3;g8
New Gloucester	E2;g7
New Limerick	B5
New Portland	D2
New Salem	D2
New Sweden	B4
New Vineyard	D2
Newburg	D3,4
Newfield	E2
Newhall	g7
Nicatous Lake (lake)	C4
Nonesuch (river)	g7
North Brother (mountain)	C4
North Guilford	C3
North Harpswell	g8
North Islesboro	D4
North Newcastle	D3
North Perry	C5
North Pond (lake)	D3
North Searsmont	D3
North Turner Mountain (mountain)	C4
North Warren	D3
North Windham	E2;g7
Norway	D2
Oakland	D3
Ogunquit	E2
Old Orchard Beach	E2;g7
Old Speck Mountain (mountain)	D2
Old Town	D4
Orono	D4
Orrington	D4
Oxford	D2
Paris	D2
Parkman	C3
Parmachenee Lake (lake)	C2
Passadumkeag Mountain (mountain)	C4
Passamaquoddy Bay (bay)	C5
Patten	C4
Peaked Mountain (mountain)	B4
Peaks Island (island)	g7
Peekaboo Mountain (mountain)	C5
Pemadumcook Lake (lake)	C3,4
Pemaquid	E3
Penobscot	D4
Penobscot Bay (bay)	D3,4
Penobscot Lake (lake)	C2
Penobscot River (river)	C,D4
Penobscot River, East Branch (river)	B,C4
Penobscot River, North Branch	B,C2,3
Penobscot River, West Branch	B,C3
Peter Dana Point	C5
Phillips	D2
Phippsburg	g8
Pierce Pond (lake)	C2
Piscataquis (river)	C3,4
Pittsfield	D3
Plaisted	A4
Pleasant (river)	C3,4
Pleasant Hill	g7
Pleasant Lake (lake)	B4
Pleasant Lake (lake)	C5
Pleasant Pond	C3
Pleasant Pond (lake)	C3
Poland Spring	D2
Popham Beach	E3
Portage	B4
Portage Lake (lake)	B4
Portland	E2;g7
Pownal Center	g7
Prentiss	C4
Presque Isle	B4
Presumpscot (river)	g7
Prouts Neck	g7
Pushaw Lake (lake)	D4
Quimby	B4
Ragged Island (island)	E4
Ragged Lake (lake)	C3
Rainbow Lake (lake)	C3
Rangeley Lake (lake)	D2
Raymond	E2;g7
Readfield	D3
Richardson Lakes (lakes)	D2
Ripogenus Lake (lake)	C3
Rockland	D3

Rockport	D3
Rocky Lake (lake)	D5
Roque Bluffs	D5
Round Pond	E3
Roxbury	D2
Royal (river)	f,g7
Rumford	D2
Rumford Corner	D2
Rump Mountain (mountain)	C1
Sabattus Pond (pond)	D2
Sabbathday Lake (lake)	g7
Saco	E2;g7
Saco (river)	E2
Saddleback Mountain (mountain)	B4
Saddleback Mountain (mountain)	D2
Saint Croix (river)	C5
Saint Croix Stream (stream)	B4
Saint David	A4
Saint Francis (river)	A3,4
Saint Froid Lake (lake)	B4
Saint John River (river)	B3;A3,4,5
Saint John River, South East Branch	B2,3
Sandy (river)	D2,3
Sandy Bay Mountain (mountain)	C2
Sanford	E2
Scarboro	E2;g7
Schoodic Lake (lake)	C4
Scraggly Lake (lake)	B4
Sebago Lake (lake)	E2;g7
Sebasticook Lake (lake)	D3
Sebec (lake)	C3
Seboeis (river)	B,C4
Seboeis Lake (lake)	B4
Seboeis Lake (lake)	C4
Seboomook Lake (lake)	B3
Shepherd Brook Mountain (mountain)	B3
Sidney	D3
Silver Lake (lake)	C3
Skowhegan	D3
Small Point	g8
Small Point (point)	g8
Snow Mountain (mountain)	C2
Snowshoe Lake (lake)	B4
Solon	D3
Sourdnahunk Lake (lake)	B3
South Berwick	E2
South Branch Lake (lake)	C4
South Deer Isle	D4
South Liberty	D3
South Lubec	D6
South Paris	D2
South Portland	E2;g7
South West Harbor	D4
Spectacle Pond (lake)	D4
Spencer Lake (lake)	C2
Spring Lake (lake)	C2
Springvale	E2
Squapan Lake (lake)	B4
Square Lake (lake)	A4
Standish	E2
State Road	B4
Stetson Mountain (mountain)	C5
Stroudwater (river)	g7
Sugarloaf Mountain (mountain)	C2
Swan Island (island)	D4
Swan Lake (lake)	D4
Sysladobsis Lake (lake)	C4
Tarkiln Hill (hill)	g7
Telos Lake (lake)	B3
Thomaston	D3
Thompson Lake (lake)	D2
Toddy Pond (lake)	D4
Topsfield	C5
Topsham	E3;g8
Troutdale	C3
Tunk Lake (lake)	D4
Turner	D2
Twin Lakes (lakes)	C4
Umbagog Lake (lake)	D1
Umculcus Lake (lake)	B4
Umsaskis Lake (lake)	B3
Union River, West Branch (river)	D4
Unionville	D5
Unity Pond (lake)	D3
Upper Wilson Pond (lake)	C3
Van Buren	A5
Vanceboro	C5
Vinalhaven Island	D4
Waite	C5
Waldoboro	D3
Walnut Hill	g7
Warren	D3
Waterboro	E2
Waterville	D3
Weld	D2
Wells	E2
Wells Beach	E2
Wesserunsatt Lake (lake)	D3
West Athens	D3
West Baldwin	E2
West Carry Pond (lake)	C2,3
West Gorham	g7
West Jonesport	D5
West Lake (lake)	C4
West Musquash Lake (lake)	C4
West Quoddy Head	D6
West Seboois	C4
Westbrook	E2;g7
White Cap Mountain (mountain)	C3
Wilson Pond (lake)	C3
Wilton	D2
Winslow	D3
Winterport	D4
Winthrop	D3
Wiscasset	D3
Wyman Dam	C3
Wyman Lake (lake)	C3
Wytopitlock	C4
Yarmouth	E2;g7
York	E2

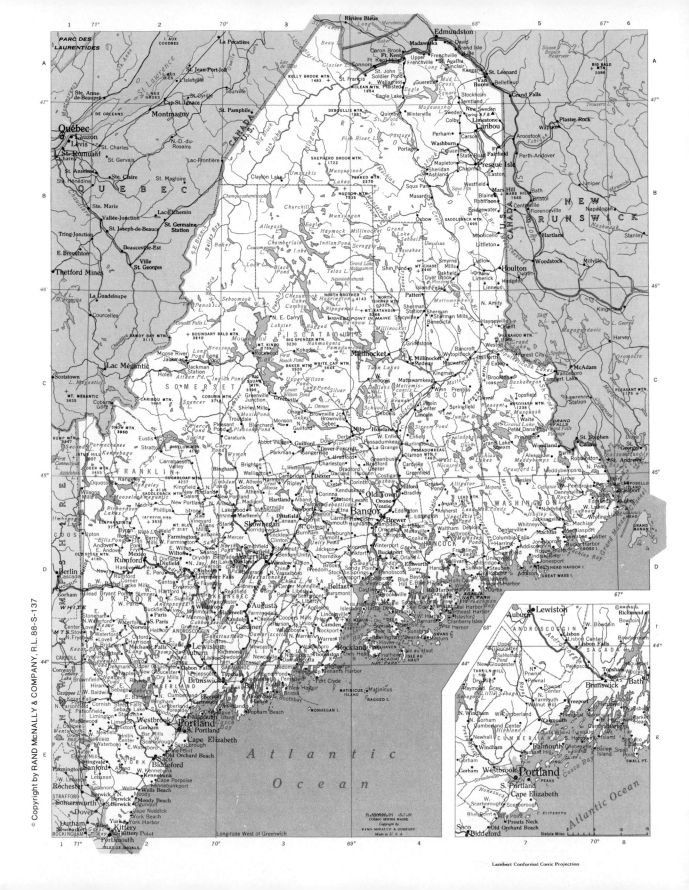

Lambert Conformal Conic Projection

FOREST PRODUCTS
DAIRY PRODUCTS
BEEF CATTLE
HOGS
POULTRY
MANUFACTURING
POTATOES
VEGETABLES
OATS
FRUIT
MAPLE SYRUP
BLUEBERRIES
MINING
FISH
LOBSTERS

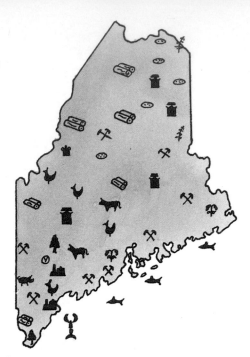

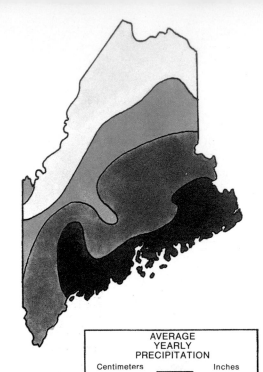

AVERAGE
YEARLY
PRECIPITATION

Centimeters		Inches
more than 112		more than 44
102 to 112		40 to 44
97 to 102		38 to 40
less than 97		less than 38

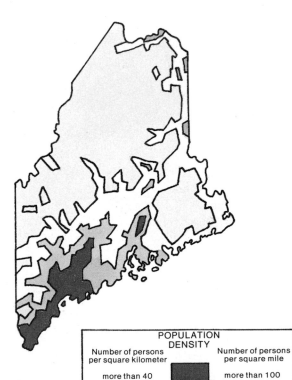

POPULATION
DENSITY

Number of persons per square kilometer		Number of persons per square mile
more than 40		more than 100
20 to 40		50 to 100
10 to 20		25 to 50
less than 10		less than 25

MAJOR
HIGHWAYS

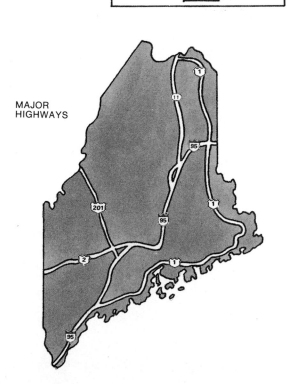

TOPOGRAPHY

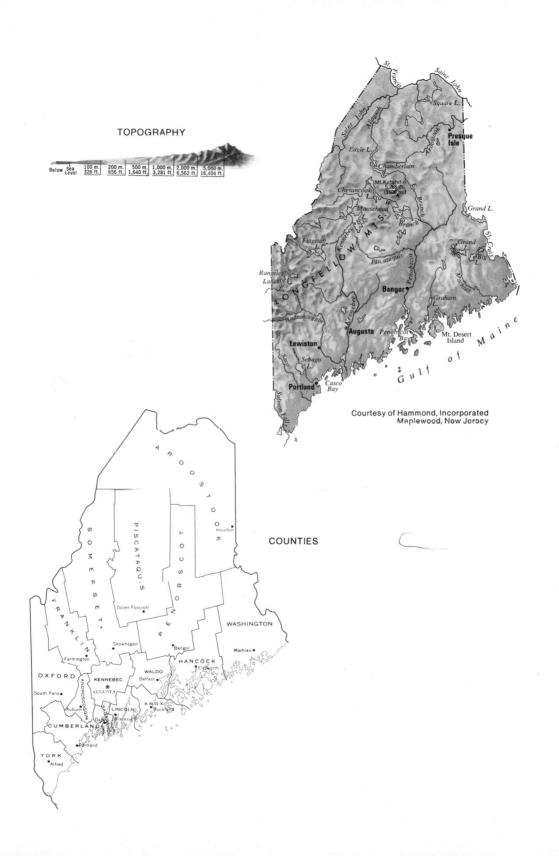

| Below Sea Level | 100 m. 328 ft. | 200 m. 656 ft. | 500 m. 1,640 ft. | 1,000 m. 3,281 ft. | 2,000 m. 6,562 ft. | 5,000 m. 16,404 ft. |

St. Francis

Saint John

Square L.

Saint John

Allagash

Aroostook

Presque Isle

Eagle L.

Chamberlain

Chesuncook L.

Mt. Katahdin 5,268 ft. 1606 m.

E. Branch

Grand L.

W. Branch

Moosehead

St. Croix

Branch

Piscataquis

Grand L.

Big L.

Flagstaff L.

Kennebec

Penobscot

Machias

Rangeley Lakes

Bangor

Graham L.

LONGFELLOW MTS.

Androscoggin

Kennebec

Mt. Desert Island

Augusta

Penobscot Bay

Gulf of Maine

Lewiston

Saco

Sebago L.

Casco Bay

Portland

Salmon Falls

Courtesy of Hammond, Incorporated
Maplewood, New Jersey

COUNTIES

A R O O S T O O K

Houlton

S O M E R S E T

P I S C A T A Q U I S

P E N O B S C O T

Dover-Foxcroft

F R A N K L I N

WASHINGTON

Skowhegan

Bangor

Machias

Farmington

HANCOCK

OXFORD

WALDO

Ellsworth

KENNEBEC

Belfast

South Paris

★ AUGUSTA

ANDROSCOGGIN

KNOX

Auburn

LINCOLN

Rockland

Damariscotta

C U M B E R L A N D

Portland

YORK

Alfred

Lobstermen's bouys are part of the tourist scene in Maine's resort villages.

INDEX

Page numbers that appear in boldface type indicate illustrations

The coast near Stonington

Picture Identifications

Front Cover: Cliffs on Mount Desert Island
Back cover: Lobster boats in the harbor, Stonington
Pages 2-3: Portland Head Light
Page 6: West Quoddy Head Lighthouse, on the easternmost point of land in the United States
Pages 8-9: Aroostook County grain field near Presque Isle
Page 20: Montage of Mainers
Pages 26-27: A Viking crew at sea
Page 38: The British cutter *Margaretta* being taken by men from Machias
Pages 44-45: *A Morning View of Blue Hill Village,* by Jonathan Fisher, 1824 (detail)
Page 54: Bath Iron Works
Page 66: The Capitol, Augusta
Pages 80-81: *Lumber Schooners at Evening on Penobscot Bay,* Fitz Hugh Lane (detail)
Pages 94-95: Tenants Harbor in the fog
Page 108: Montage showing the state flag, state tree (white pine), state bird (chickadee), state insect (honeybee), state flower (white pinecone and tassel), and state mineral (tourmaline)
Page 126: The coast at Ogunquit

About the Author

Ty Harrington, writer-photographer, is author of *The Last Cathedral,* which received the Book of the Year award from the English-Speaking Union; *The Sailing Chef;* and *Never Too Old.* A former staff member of the *National Geographic* and a worldwide traveler with expertise in the Amazon and Polar regions, he has written and contributed to many articles. He also serves as an officer with the Federal Emergency Management Agency, assisting in presidentially declared disasters such as hurricanes, earthquakes, and tornadoes. Mr. Harrington makes his home in Wilton, Connecticut.

Picture Acknowledgments

Odyssey Productions: © Robert Frerck: Front cover
SuperStock International: Back cover, 23 (left), 100 (right), 103
Photo Options: © Chuck Snow Photo, Inc.: 2-3, 11; © Kenny Walters: 17 (top right); © Renae Hewitt: 23 (right); © Michael Philip Manheim: 75 (middle)
Shostal Associates: 13, 15, 76 (bottom left), 106 (right), 108 (honeybee), 122; © Jim Kraus: 4; © George Goodwin: 64; © Patrick W. Grace: 83 (left), 118 (right), 126; © Suzanne J. Engelmann: 105
Root Resources: © Kitty Kohout: 5, 106 (left), 108 (pinecone), 113 (left); © Voscar The Maine Photographer: 8-9, 12, 19, 20 (middle left), 65, 71 (top left, bottom right), 74 (left), 119 (top middle), 123; © Lia Munson: 17 (bottom right); © Dean Abramson: 71 (top right), 72, 97 (bottom), 98 (left), 99, 119 (top right), 141; © Earl L. Kubis: 76 (top right); © James Blank: 76 (bottom right); © Mary Ann Hemphill: 100 (left); © Ted Farrington: 113 (top right)
Photri: 6, 75 (left), 84 (top right), 116; © Joe Atchison: 76 (middle right); © B. Kulik: 101
North Wind Picture Archives: 30, 56 (right), 61 (middle), 62 (right), 79, 128 (top), 131 (Samantha Smith); © Jim Scourletis: 14 (both pictures), 84 (bottom right); photo courtesy L.L. Bean, Inc.: 127
© **Jerry Hennen:** 16 (left), 108 (chickadee), 113 (top middle)
TSW-Click/Chicago: © Willard Clay: 16 (right); © Jon Feingersh: 76 (middle left), 108 (trees); © Raymond G. Barnes: 102 (right)
© **Lynn M. Stone:** 17 (top left, top middle, bottom left), 113 (bottom middle)
© **Jeff Greenberg:** 20 (top left, top middle, top right, middle right), 22, 34, 56 (left), 74 (right), 83 (right), 84 (left), 85, 102 (left), 121
Porterfield/Chickering: 20 (bottom left, bottom right), 49, 104, 120 (all three pictures)
The Granger Collection: 26-27, 31 (left), 32 (both pictures), 42, 47, 86 (left), 87 (left, right), 112, 125, 129 (Jewett and Fuller), 130 (Millay and Nordica), 131 (top)
The Bettmann Archive, Inc.: 31 (right), 51, 88 (middle left), 128 (Bush), 129 (Gilbreth), 130 (Maxim and Robinson)
Historical Pictures Service, Chicago: 35, 38, 88 (middle right), 128 (Curtis)
Collections of the Maine Historical Society: 36 (detail), 41 (detail), 48, 53, 57 (both pictures, details), 61 (top left, top right, bottom, details), 62 (left, middle), 91 (top left, detail)
Collection of William A. Farnsworth Library and Art Museum: 44-45
The National Archives: 52 (inset)
Courtesy of Scribner, New York: 52 (Gettysburg battle scene)
Journalism Services: © John Patsch: 54
Marilyn Gartman Agency: © G.A. Reims: 66, 138; © Michael Philip Manheim: 75 (right), 91 (middle left, bottom right), 118 (left), 119 (left, middle right, bottom right)
Maine Department of Economic Development: 68
Maine Office of Tourism: 71 (middle left, middle right, bottom left), 86 (right), 91 (bottom left), 97 (top), 98 (right), 115, 117
Cameramann International Ltd.: 76 (top left)
National Gallery of Art, Washington; Andrew W. Mellon Fund and Gift of Mr. and Mrs. Francis W. Hatch, Sr.: 80-81 (detail)
AP/Wide World Photos, Inc.: 87 (middle), 128 (Chase), 129 (Kent), 131 (White and Whitney), 132
Wadsworth Atheneum, Hartford. The Ella Gallup Sumner and Mary Catlin Sumner Collection: 88 (top right, detail)
Museum of Fine Arts, Boston: M. and M. Karolik Collection: 88 (bottom, detail); Seth K. Sweetser Fund, Tompkins Collection, Henry H. and Zoe Oliver Sherman Fund and Gift of Mrs. R. Amory Thorndike: 88 (top left, detail)
© **Joseph A. DiChello, Jr.:** 91 (top right), 94-95
© **Jerome Wyckoff:** 108 (tourmaline)
Tom Stack & Associates: © Don & Pat Valenti: 110
© **James P. Rowan:** 113 (bottom right)
Len W. Meents: Maps on 97, 101, 103, 105, 136
Courtesy Flag Research Center, Winchester, Massachusetts 01890: Flag on 108